THE LIGHT TRAVELERS

To ROLAND,
WISHING YOU ALL THE BEST
ON YOUR JOURNEY —
HOPE YOU ENJOY THE RIDE ⌣
ALL THE BEST,

THE LIGHT TRAVELERS

A MYSTICAL JOURNEY

NICK ATLAS, PHD

EVOLUTIONARY®
EDUCATION

Published by:
Evolutionary Education, LLC.
Villa Rica, Georgia USA
evolutionaryeducation.org
nickatlas.com
thelighttravelers.com

ISBN 978-1-7332935-0-1 (Paperback)
ISBN 978-1-7332935-1-8 (Ebook - EPUB)
ISBN 978-1-7332935-2-5 (EBook - Mobi)

Library of Congress Control Number: 2019909744

Printed in the United States of America

NOTE: This book occasionally describes the author's experimentation with psilocybin mushrooms and altered states of consciousness more generally. It is a criminal offense in the United States and in many other countries, punishable by imprisonment and/or fines, to manufacture, possess, or supply psilocybin, except in connection with government-sanctioned research. This book is not intended for you to break the law. The author and the publisher expressly disclaim any liability, loss, or risk, personal or otherwise, that is incurred as a consequence, directly or indirectly, of the contents of this book.

Certain names and locations have been changed in order to protect the author and others.

Cover art by GDJ.

FOR MARY ELLEN AND STEPHEN

Once upon a time I dreamt I was a butterfly, fluttering hither and thither, to all intents and purposes a butterfly. I was conscious only of my happiness as a butterfly, unaware that I was a man. Soon I awaked, and there I was, veritably myself again. Now I do not know whether I was then a man dreaming I was a butterfly, or whether I am now a butterfly dreaming I am a man.

- Chuang Tzu, c. 300 BCE

THE LIGHT TRAVELERS

PROLOGUE

WHEN I WAS TWENTY-ONE YEARS OLD, I fell in love with the most beautiful woman I had ever met. Within a year of our meeting, she was hit by a car in a hotel parking lot on Halloween night.

I was at work when I learned of her accident. A mutual friend told me over the phone as I looked down over Park Avenue from my small office in a busy law firm. She had suffered a catastrophic brain injury and was in a coma.

I shared the news in an online forum that had increasingly become the most intimate community in my life. Several members of the forum suggested that when I next visited her, everyone would send their prayers at a prearranged time and I would serve as the anchor. I had never done anything like that before, but what did I have to lose?

In January, two months after her accident, I visited her at a hospital in Atlanta, Georgia. When I saw her lying there, unconscious, time slowed down. That afternoon, we wheeled her into a large room, empty except for a few other patients, some bare tables, and a television against the wall. Sitting across from her, as the clock struck five I closed my eyes and began to concentrate. Within moments I found myself encompassed by a radiant blue light that eventually took the shape of a sphere. My body grew extremely hot. I then attempted to direct the light into her.

She didn't wake up from her coma for another seven months. After the visit, I returned to New York and began writing this book in her honor. Within half a year I quit my job, hit the road, and followed my heart into the unknown.

The stories you are about to read are personal and, in many cases, obscure. At times, you may have to suspend doubt and disbelief, just as I did. It has been a wonderful challenge to try to express the inexpressible. While several character names have been changed, I've done my best to share the experiences of my journey as faithfully as possible. Life is so fragile and our time on Earth so precious; I'm grateful that you've chosen to spend some time with me.

CHAPTER 1
AWAKENING

CORETTA NEVER GOT ANGRY. Having grown up in New York, I didn't know anyone that wasn't at least a little bit cynical, so I figured she was repressing her emotions and that sooner or later she would explode.

"It's my faith," she confided in me one morning.

We were on an island off the coast of Belize, walking side-by-side along the rocks in search of a hidden waterfall.

"I feel God with me always," she said.

When we found the waterfall, she reached into her bag and pulled out a bikini. Removing her light blue tank top and a small, turtle pendant she wore around her neck, she covered her breasts with her forearm and flashed a mischievous grin.

"You better turn around or you're gonna see a whole lotta sunshine!"

I hid my eyes for fear of going blind.

Our bungalow, which we shared with another companion from our study abroad program, was undoubtedly haunted. Coretta and Elizabeth took the ant-infested cots while I tossed and turned with only a thin blanket against the creaky, hardwood floors. We spent a few sleepless nights listening to whispers through the cracks and the incessant drip of a leaky faucet.

Then, one afternoon, the front door slammed shut behind us as we exited, locking us out. Taking it as a sign, the three of us decided we'd had enough and caught the next speedboat back to the mainland in preparation for the coming week's classes. It was the morning of September 11th, 2001, and we were running late.

Arriving at the bus station in Belize City, we huddled around a small television as the twin towers crumbled to the ground. I pictured my father riding in the first car of the subway streaking toward the courthouses down by City Hall. He had done it every weekday for twenty years, only now the scene was engulfed in flames. I stared at the screen. Coretta held me close.

Later, my parents called to let me know they were alright. I didn't pick up the phone. I was too busy dancing with Coretta around a raging fire.

We spent weeks at a time in the jungle and occasionally traveled back and forth between the mainland and the cayes. I confessed my love to Coretta one night on the beach beneath the full moon after I had smiled at her and she'd said that my crooked teeth looked perfect.

"I'm falling for you, too," she said, "but I'm still in love with my boyfriend back home."

From then on, we kept a safe distance from each other and ultimately went our separate ways. I settled in a small, seaside village occupied by Garifuna, an Afro-indigenous ethnic group native to the Caribbean. Former slaves, the Garifuna are one of a handful of peoples whose language, rich heritage and traditional practices, like subsistence fishing and farming, survived the cruel hand of colonialism.

In the village, on most days I rose at 5:00 am to fish out along the reef from a sleek, yellow kayak lent to me by my landlord. I usually didn't catch anything, but one particularly still November morning I caught at least ten fish, including a shiny speckled grouper as large as my thigh. I knew this because I had to shove it in the space between my legs where it flopped around, slowly suffocating beside all the others. When I reached land, Thomas, who I spent many an afternoon with, was there to greet me with a bottle of kerosene and a greased skillet.

"I'll be damned, white boy!" he exclaimed. "Look at you! A fisher-man!"

Thomas was short and spry, with sinewy muscles and a lean jaw and cheekbones. He always wore a black leather, spitfire cap, a tight, white tank top, slacks and sandals. A self-identified Rastafarian wood carver, his electric gray eyes bulged with vitality. He lived across the road in a one-room shack with his wife, an Australian expat, and their two young children. He constantly smoked cannabis rolled in loose-leaf paper and once, when he'd exhausted his notebook, tore a page from the Qur'an to roll a joint. I was aghast!

"Don't worry," he insisted. "It's a blank page! Ha! I-Mon never defame the word of *Al-lah*!"

As Thomas whittled small objects out of driftwood, which he would sell to the rare tourist, I would listen.

"You know something, white boy? I'm a prophet! Ha! A prophet! I pull messages out the wood. I prophesize!"

"Oh yeah?" I said. "If you're a prophet, what am I supposed to do with my life?" I came from a family of lawyers and, as none of my siblings had followed suit, I assumed it was up to me to carry the torch. The thought filled me with dread.

"Listen here," he said, jutting his chin at me. "I'll tell you a secret. You need to find yourself a *cave*, boy! Ha! That's right, a cave! Someplace where *Babylon* won't find you while they're hunting Bin Laden!"

The locals were fond of referring to the Western establishment as "Babylon" and, after 9/11, had taken to calling everyone they didn't trust "Bin Laden." They joked about the latter constantly with me, as I had grown a beard since I'd arrived, and no one knew why I was there or when I would leave.

"One day, you'll remember me," he said. "You'll remember me while you're sitting in your cave and the bombs are blowing up outside. You'll remember this moment when I spoke the truth to you. Ha! Prophesize!"

That was Thomas, forever spinning a yarn while his hands and eyes delved deeper into his woodwork. One afternoon, he found out I had a TV in my bungalow. He came inside to watch sitcoms but was more interested in the commercials. Transfixed, within minutes he had nearly sliced off his finger but only damaged a small pipe he'd been carving for two days straight.

"Shiiiiiiiiiittttttttttt," he said with a crooked, embarrassed smirk smeared across his chiseled face.

The sun went up, the sun went down. The tide came in, the tide rolled out.

When Thomas saw me registering for classes online, he laughed.

"You're a slave, white boy!"

"A slave?"

"That's right! A slave. A slave to the Babylon system!"

"I'm just trying to sign up for school so I can get started on my thesis," I said.

Dissatisfied, he smacked his lips in defiance.

"You're a slave," he repeated. "You just don't know it yet."

I had planned to write a research paper on traditional, Garifuna fishing practices and had hoped to spend the bulk of the month at sea. Upon settling in, however, I'd learned that very few fishermen were left since the ecotourism industry had descended upon Belize, luring young men into "lucrative" careers as bartenders and towel boys. Having spent the month on the beach with Thomas instead, and with a deadline fast approaching, I turned to him for counsel.

"What do I do?"

"Speak the truth," he said, raising a thick, bushy eyebrow at me. His wide eyes pierced my own and my skin bristled.

Retreating to my tiny bungalow, I reread my notes, studied the interviews I had collected and relived the most penetrating moments of my time in the village.

7

I recalled a discouraged, old farmer.

"The youth have abandoned our customs," he'd said.

A thoughtful, young man had added, "We're losing our vernacular. What will become of us?"

I remembered the children laughing in the streets, the young girls whispering in each other's ears, and their mothers huddled around a deceased sister, moaning night after night after night.

*   *   *

I returned to Georgia the following January and school began a week later. Seeking an easy ride my final semester, I'd enrolled in a course entitled "Mind/Body Healing." The class was taught by Geshela, a tranquil, Tibetan *lama* who draped himself in saffron robes each day. Looking into his twinkling brown eyes felt like standing in the warm sun.

During that first week back, my exuberant ex-girlfriend, Penelope, told me to seek out someone she had met while I was away—a lanky, dread-locked, easy-going guy from Florida named Devon, who was also in his senior year.

"You don't know Devon!?" she said.

"Why would I know Devon?"

"Because you're so much alike, minus the hair."

Devon had enrolled in "Mind/Body Healing," too, and we hit it off immediately. Inspired by Geshela, we began researching the "Bodhisattva vow"—dedicating one's life to the enlightenment of others—and ways to cure illness through

8

meditation. Geshela had also begun to guide us into deep states of relaxation at the end of our classes. Occasionally, I felt like I was floating up and out of my body, and sometimes vibrant colors would completely consume me. My whole world would be orange or violet and utterly serene for a few, delicious moments. Then, one night, I had a dream that caused me to shoot up in bed. In the morning, I recorded it in a small notebook I kept on the nightstand:

> *Last night I was shot in the center of my forehead and died. I experienced a period of nothingness before being reborn through a birth canal and emerging into a bright green hospital room. I thought that I was still in my previous body, but it may have been a memory of what I was like before. Something has shifted, though I'm not sure what.*

For spring break, Devon and I loaded up my car and drove through Florida, camping along the way. As we traveled we read Carlos Castaneda, which Devon had introduced me to, and discussed healing: what exactly did this mean and how could we learn to do it?

A few days into the trip, we met up with three of his friends from home in a stretch of forest situated between the silt-brown Suwannee river and a handful of crystal clear, natural springs. There were cardinals, bright red, singing in the trees all around the small clearing where we gathered.

Together, the five of us ate magic mushrooms and sat listening to the birds until, one by one, we began to wander.

I walked through the woods to an oak grove littered with white lilies and swallowtail butterflies floating along the grass. I felt like I had entered into an impressionist painting. I'd taken mushrooms before. In the past, I might have panicked. But this time, I embraced my disorientation, spun myself around to further lose my bearings, flopped down on the ground, and imagined myself in the Garden of Eden. I felt the distance between myself and the Earth evaporate.

After several minutes, I rose. I could feel the squirrels and small burrowing animals moving underfoot as I walked the land in my socks, which got soaked with dew. Arriving at a barbed-wire fence that marked the property line, I was gripped with sadness. An arbitrary boundary seemed so ridiculous. How could the Earth, no longer separate from my own body, be owned?

Finding my way back to the clearing, I decided to try to meditate. During our road trip, Devon had started reading a book by Timothy Leary, an author I'd never heard of, who suggested that we take psychedelic drugs and focus our minds "inward." Sitting down between the roots of two adjacent oak trees, I leaned back into an enormous trunk alongside the edge of the lazy river and closed my eyes. A moment later, I perceived a shimmering golden light in the center of my forehead, in the same area where I had been shot in my dream a month or so earlier. As my breath steadied and mind stilled, the light expanded into a luminous tunnel. I followed it, as if I were moving toward its nexus. Then, in an instant, an incredible sensation erupted in my loins and surged throughout my body in all directions, like an orgasm but exponentially stronger. I was spellbound.

When I pried myself from the tree, the powerful rushes of energy still swirling through me, the whole group reassembled in the clearing as if by design. Soon the skies turned the color of charcoal and a huge thunderstorm barreled in from the south, drenching everyone to the bone.

As the rain pounded down upon us and the group ran for cover, Devon and I didn't budge, determined to take the full brunt of the storm. At one point it felt as if we were raising its intensity with our minds, pushing each other toward a deeper experience of union.

In the days and weeks that followed, I felt a wonderful sense of radiance. I could also feel the eyes of others inspecting me and found that I could attract their attention simply by looking at them. At times, I was convinced I could "hear" their thoughts in my mind before they were spoken. Though the surges of energy in my body had largely subsided, I occasionally felt strange, vibratory sensations in my palms, forehead and spine, as if someone were tickling me with a feather.

Devon and I graduated in May and wore old t-shirts and flip-flops under our caps and gowns. I had my headphones on throughout most of the ceremony, except during a commencement speech by the mathematician Benoit Mandelbrot, who received an honorary degree and whose name was familiar to me as there was a screensaver named after him. My ears perked up when Dr. Mandelbrot digressed from his perplexing explanation of fractal dynamics, the tone of his voice deepening slightly.

"Behold the *word* and the weight it carries," he said. "Words can hold you captive, or they can set you free."

My mind flashed back to Thomas sitting on the beach whittling small bowls out of driftwood.

"Speak the truth," he'd said. "Speak the truth."

CHAPTER 2
SYNCHRONICITY

EMANCIPATED, DEVON AND I eyed music festivals across the country. We focused on one in particular: Bonnaroo, outside Nashville, Tennessee. In the interim, I moved back in with my parents in New York City and took a job as a law clerk. My boss was an old partner of my father's and, thankfully, he was exceptionally lenient with me, allowing me unpaid vacations at my leisure.

"I make extra money when you're here," he said, peering out from behind a mountain of paperwork. "But, I don't lose any when you're not. Besides, you're only young once."

I took full advantage of this policy and booked my tickets for Bonnaroo right from my office desk on the 16th floor. In the days prior to leaving I was looking out through the massive windows at Park Avenue and all the busy ants of midtown scurrying about with their cell phones, briefcases and take-out sushi boxes, when I received an unexpected phone call from Coretta. We hadn't spoken in months.

"Are you going to Bonnaroo?" she asked after we'd caught up.

"I just bought my ticket!" I exclaimed. My heart was racing now, nearly beating out of my chest.

"I'll be there too!" she said, elated.

And with that we hung up. It was settled. We'd meet at Bonnaroo.

When it came time for the festival, I flew back down to Georgia where I met up with Devon and Penelope. We drove to Tennessee through an excruciating heat wave. After several hellacious hours we peeled out of Devon's station wagon and situated ourselves in a large camp with other friends from school who were already celebrating our new lease on life. The festival was enormous. Soon, the grounds began to swell, and it became challenging to navigate the sea of revelers. As there wasn't any cell phone service, it was virtually impossible to find anyone intentionally.

The weekend cruised along with no sign of Coretta. The temperature continued to soar, and a number of performers incorporated rain dances into their shows. Without a cloud in the sky, however, a cool, cleansing downpour seemed as unlikely as tracking down the woman of my dreams. Fortunately, Coretta wasn't the only reason I'd come to Bonnaroo.

Sound Tribe Sector 9 had caught my attention the previous spring after Penelope had given me a recording of one of their shows. It was unlike anything I had ever heard. She and I had become enamored with the Atlanta rave scene a few years earlier, frequently staying up all night to dance. Sound Tribe had tapped into the same energy, driving bass lines and heart-pounding rhythms, only they used live instruments and had a style all their own.

A group of five, they played under the stars each night at Bonnaroo. Large, glittering quartz and amethyst crystals adorned the stage. The band's core followers stood nearby, many of them clutching smaller crystals in their hands and wearing cryptic symbols on their clothing or on chains clasped around their necks. Curious what the symbols meant, I turned to a woman next to me. Her eyes were wide.

"Time is art," she said. "The symbols represent a shift in the way we measure time."

Prior to leaving their final show at Bonnaroo, I stood absolutely still for a moment and thought hard about my own relationship to time, envisioning my ideal future. I imagined traveling to festivals around the world to document the freedom and euphoria characteristic of these fleeting paradises. I wanted to photograph people experiencing transcendence through drumming, dancing, and nomadic living. Above all else, I wanted to keep dancing outdoors, which had quickly become the most important thing in my life. This was one possibility anyway, which I wrote down on a scrap of paper and stuffed inside my wallet amidst old receipts and some leftover Belizean dollars.

"Don't be afraid to take the road less traveled," said a voice from beside me.

I turned to see a short, round, jolly figure with twinkling brown eyes and an infectious smile.

"Excuse me?" I said.

"I saw what you wrote," he said. "I remember when I was your age. I did exactly the same thing."

I nodded, slightly embarrassed.

"My name is Rob Newton," he said.

He extended a hand the size of a cantaloupe but shook mine gently.

"Pleased to meet you," I said. I noticed he had a backstage pass on a lanyard hanging from his neck. "Are you a musician?"

"I've been known to play a little bit," he said.

I suddenly had the feeling that I was in the presence of greatness and grew quiet. Rather than forcing conversation, we stood in silence with our eyes closed for several minutes just "being." I could feel energy stirring in my heart. Finally, Rob spoke up.

"That was excellent," he said.

"What was *that?*"

"That was the 'Now.' The eternal, present moment, and we were there together. I've been living in the Now for over twenty years. Surfing the Universe, listening to it implicitly and hanging out in the small crack of time just on the cusp of creation."

His presence seemed to hold me still as he spoke, and my eyes lit up to match his.

"What do you mean?" I said. I had occasionally overheard people talking about "living in the Now," but it was new to me and I didn't understand what they were referring to.

Without warning, Rob moved within inches of my face and thrust his hands toward me as if to break down any sense of personal space. "The Now. Right now. Here, in this moment!" he said with increasing intensity.

Shivers rushed up and down my spine and I started shaking uncontrollably, as if reality had been amplified.

"You *feel* me?" he said. He smiled as he turned down the volume and backed off a bit.

"Uh huh," I said, still quivering.

"You see, my life changed one day when I was in Japan. I was walking down the street and felt the sudden urge to run to the aid of an unharmed woman, but I hesitated. I didn't trust my intuition, and in the next instant I watched her fall. I was so sad. I felt like I'd failed. I vowed never to let that happen again and have followed my heart in every moment ever since, even when people think I'm craaaaaayyyyzzzzzeeee."

"I think I can relate," I said. "Things started to change for me a few months ago. It's like the lights turned on inside me, and now my body feels like an antenna. It's a little overwhelming."

"You're pretty thin, so you must have a 'sensitive' body type," he said. "I've got a friend who feels energy just like you do."

"What about you? Do you feel it?" I looked up and down his teddy bear physique.

"Nope," he said, smiling brightly. "I *know* the vibe, but I don't feel it. It has its advantages, but no more than yours. We all have our gifts. The important thing is that we share them. They fit together like puzzle pieces. Speaking of which, have you heard of the 'hundredth monkey?'"

17

"No."

"So, these scientists, right? They had this experiment in which they taught a skill to a bunch of monkeys and as soon as the hundredth monkey learned it, they all got it!"

"Spontaneously?" I asked.

"Yep. It's called *morphic resonance*. The basic idea is that consciousness spreads through the ether like wildfire." As he told the story he grew more and more excited. "Humans will have a similar evolution to a different plane of non-physical, luminous existence once the threshold has been reached."

"Any idea when this is going to happen?" Since my experience of golden light beneath the oak trees, I had begun to accept a lot of things I'd never thought were possible, but I maintained a healthy skepticism of this claim.

"Beats me," said Rob, "but I believe it in my bones."

Eager to hear more of his theories, I tried to keep the conversation alive.

"What about music?" I asked. "What do you play? Bass?" He struck me as a bass player, unshakable.

"Ha! The bass is my mistress," he said, pausing as if reminiscing of her fondly. "But the guitar... the guitar's my destiny."

I felt shivers rush through me once again.

"What's your destiny, young man?" His eyes seemed to penetrate mine like lasers.

I shrugged.

Rob smiled back at me. "Don't worry about it," he said. "You've got time. Just remember, reality is a little bigger than you think. Speaking of which, angels have been watching over us all weekend."

He pointed toward the sky. Sure enough, one of the fluffy white clouds overhead had taken the perfect form of a winged deity. I watched it dance across an ocean of stars for a few moments, wondering if it really was an angel. When I looked back down, Rob was gone.

By mid-afternoon on the last day of the festival, Penelope and I were indulging in each other's company over a bottle of red wine. Béla Fleck, the legendary banjo maestro, serenaded us with classical music in the background and life felt bubbly—precisely how she liked it. We knew the moment wouldn't last, but we were determined to marinate in it as long as we could.

"Stop looking at me like that," she said, blushing.

"Like what?"

Thunder crackled overhead. The rainstorm everyone had been hoping for arrived to curtail the heat and keep the rising dust at bay. The two of us were completely drenched. Once the storm passed, Penelope and I wandered together through the steaming wet grass toward the main stage, surrounded by fifty thousand soggy, jovial young people awaiting the festival's headliners, the Grateful Dead. "The Dead" were performing for the first time since their legendary front man, Jerry Garcia, had died a few years earlier. As they took the stage, the massive crowd let out a deafening roar. At that exact moment, I felt someone brush up against me from behind and wheeled around to see who it was.

19

"Coretta!" I was shocked and, from the looks of it, so was she.

"I knew we'd find each other," she said.

A wave of bliss swept over us. In an instant, Penelope vanished into the crowd. As she disappeared, it seemed as if an entire phase of my life abruptly ended, and another one began. The whimsical sounds of the Dead's classic tune "Sugar Magnolia" rang out from the stage. Coretta took my hand.

"Care to dance?" she said.

I nodded, closing my eyes. All the feelings I'd bottled up came flooding back. The thing was, her boyfriend, Jonathan, was there too, standing behind us. He didn't interrupt.

After several minutes, the song ended. I wanted to stay, but I knew I couldn't. I gave Coretta a necklace of flowers I had made for her, kissed her on the forehead, and drifted away with the tide.

CHAPTER 3
THE HEALER

IT WAS A LONELY AUTUMN in New York City. I sat with my back to the 16th floor windows of the same, stale Park Avenue office where I drank third-rate coffee mixed with generic hot cocoa and stared at a computer screen for hours on end. Trapped in an oversized filing cabinet and nursing a heavy heart, I felt like a caged bird. I had no idea when I'd see Coretta again.

I was kept company by Carlos Castaneda's books, which I consumed feverishly, and Sound Tribe's Internet message board, the "Lowdown," where everybody from the scene stayed in touch. Initially, I chose an anonymous handle just to feel it out, as online forums were a relatively new phenomenon in 2002, and I didn't know what to expect.

One day, I made the mistake of teasing Penelope, who was also on the Lowdown, about an argument we'd had over the summer. I was immediately reprimanded by several people for introducing passive-aggressive negativity and quickly learned that the Lowdown was no ordinary forum. Contributors often chose inventive monikers and were encouraged to post thoughts pertaining to music, dreams, mystical experiences, wellness and literature; to share original poetry, creative writing, and community-based projects; to set up ride-sharing opportunities; and, above all else, to keep the vibe positive.

Day after day I checked-in with this virtual collective. Over the course of a few months, I connected with a number of intelligent, vibrant and enthusiastic, albeit somewhat new age people sitting at various office desks, coffee shops, dining room tables and log cabins across the country. All of us yearned for the next gathering. I had hoped to find Rob Newton on there, but I never did.

Sound Tribe continued to tour relentlessly despite the festival season having ended, and every day there were new posts about synchronicities—seemingly meaningful coincidences similar to the one I had experienced when I'd bumped into Coretta at Bonnaroo. Occasionally someone would recount a visionary dream in which they were visited by wise spirits, deceased relatives offering advice and, more often than not, by the band members themselves. Before long, *I* was receiving dreamtime visits from Sound Tribe Sector 9 and was befriending complete strangers at dream concerts, "astral" festivals and in pristine yet unfamiliar natural settings. Large quartz crystals, like the ones the band placed onstage during their performances, also found their way into my nightly sojourns, as did increasing amounts of audible and, at times, visceral music. Impossible feats like flying, telepathy and shape shifting into animals became regular occurrences. On some nights I swore I was actually looking-in on a live performance at a nightclub in one city or another. Upon waking, my recollection of entire scenes was so vivid that I began to keep a dream journal beside my pillow and would write steadfastly throughout the night and nearly every morning. All I had to do was remember a single detail and a whole adventure would uncoil itself like a ball of yarn.

As Halloween approached, plans were made to attend Sound Tribe's costume party at a large music hall in Atlanta. When the time came I flew south once again and rendezvoused with Devon, who had driven up from Florida. I had invited Coretta to join us, but she'd turned us down in favor of seeing her favorite band, Widespread Panic, who were an institution amongst Southern youths.

About a week later, having returned to work in New York, I received an unexpected call from Elizabeth, our roommate while studying abroad in Belize. I immediately knew something was wrong.

"Did you hear about Coretta?" Her tone was grim.

"No."

"She was in an accident."

The world stopped.

"What happened?" I asked.

"She was hit by a car outside her hotel after the concert on Halloween."

"Where is she?"

"She's in a coma at a special hospital in Atlanta. She's barely hanging on. Sorry to have to tell you this. I just found out."

The walls of my office were caving in on me.

I got on the phone, tracked down her family and spoke with her mother, Jocelyn, for the first time since I'd known her daughter. She told me through her tears that Coretta's brain

23

damage was substantial and that her father, a prominent doctor in their hometown of Savannah, had suggested the chances of her ever recovering were slim to none.

Days and weeks passed. Coretta remained comatose, showing no signs of waking up. Still in shock, I distracted myself by researching alternative methods of healing, figuring there was nothing left to lose. Since I spent most days wasting time behind my desk or watching the ants on the street and had little social life to speak of, my support network was the Lowdown. I shared the news of Coretta's accident and asked for help. Within a few days, I had received an overwhelming response. Devon, in particular, messaged me nearly every day with encouragement. He was adamant about conducting an experiment in healing.

His idea was for me to visit Coretta, sit beside her and serve as an anchor for healing energy while the other members of the Lowdown projected it out at a specific date and time. Everyone I knew supported the idea, including Coretta's family, my parents, coworkers, and many self-professed nonbelievers. I booked a plane ticket to Georgia for the first week of January, which was Coretta's birthday.

When I arrived in Atlanta I met up with Elizabeth, who lived in Colorado and timed her visit with mine. We went to see Coretta together. She was unconscious, disfigured, and her limbs moved involuntarily like an infant's. She seemed to emit an inexplicable radiance. My eyes traced her vibrant yet nearly lifeless body. I was overcome with emotion. Rather than feeling sad or defeated, I felt energized and inspired. For hours

24

we held her hands, spoke to her softly and told her family about the strength we knew she still possessed. It was as if the shining person we all were in love with was there deep inside her body, only she was curled up in a little ball like a scared child.

When we left the hospital, Elizabeth and I headed to a small nightclub in Decatur in an effort to meet up with Devon. He happened to be in Atlanta for the weekend, having driven up from Florida to visit some relatives. We had made tentative plans to find each other at the club, but, as he didn't have a cell phone, we weren't sure how it would work out.

A few minutes after Elizabeth and I arrived at the club, a voice rang out over the P.A.: "Will 'Nick the Healer' please come to the front of the room. There's someone waiting to meet you."

A jolt of energy shot up my spine as I searched for the source of the message echoing through me. I'd never thought of myself as a healer. Moving toward the stage, a single idea poured forth from my tingling mind as the seas parted beside the bar.

We're all healers and have a magical potential lying dormant inside us, waiting to be discovered and developed.

Devon appeared before me. When we locked eyes and embraced, I felt like I was reconnecting with a long-lost friend—a soul mate. It felt like we had known each other forever, and that we'd met each other for a reason.

"Good luck tomorrow," he said. "We're all behind you."

I barely slept that night. At 5:00 p.m. the next day, the time that had been designated for the healing session, I sat beside Coretta. She was slumped in a wheelchair in a large, bright, common area within the hospital. The sound of an old TV echoed quietly in the background. Elizabeth and Jocelyn, Coretta's mother, sat across from us. No one knew what to expect.

A shift in my consciousness, a distinct feeling of being "locked-in," happened abruptly and with tremendous force. I didn't know if I had programmed myself to do it, or if the astounding magnitude of all those who were praying from afar set it in motion. I'd hardly meditated at all since my awakening beneath the oak trees in Florida and had almost no frame of reference with which to navigate inner landscapes. Steadying my breath, my body slowly relaxed.

After a few moments my upturned hands settled upon my knees. At the advice of my friends from the Lowdown, in my left palm I clasped a small piece of rose quartz crystal. Recalling Geshela's lessons, I gathered a vision of Avalokiteshvara—the Buddhist embodiment of compassion—calling forth rainbow-colored, healing light from all the Buddhas and Bodhisattvas of the Universe. I then imagined channeling the blue light of compassion out of my heart and into Coretta's body. I felt a bit like a child playing make-believe, but I did my best to cast aside doubt.

I began to feel subtle, electrical currents filling my body, starting at my feet and working their way up my legs, hands, arms, and torso until I was vibrating all over. At some point, however, I sensed that I needed to shift my body slightly, so I cupped my hands in my lap like a bowl. The impact was immediate, as electricity raced up my arms and into my head, nearly knocking me over. Energy surged up and down my spine and formed a circuit around my arms. I'd become a highly charged sphere of light extending far beyond my physical body.

Extending my hands over Coretta, I attempted to remove the blocked energy I had perceived in her, and to draw her out from the depths. I'd never trained in energy healing and wasn't sure if I was actually helping her, but it was happening *through* me, so I didn't stop to question it. There was immense pressure in my hands as they moved back and forth a few inches above her writhing body. I could feel my temperature rising, and my jaw began to churn like a cow's chewing cud. At some point I heard, as if through a tube that had remained connected to the hospital room, Elizabeth and Jocelyn expressing their concern over the beads of sweat that had formed across my face. Sensing their fear, I slowly opened my eyes, started to let-up and, sighing with relief, gradually turned to look at the clock on the wall. It read 5:35 p.m. I had been in a trance for thirty-five minutes but hadn't been aware of the passage of time at all. Hot and disoriented, I drank some water and ate a little stale bread. A sudden, unexpected swell of anger boiled inside me.

How could no one have told me that I have this ability? I thought. *That we all do?*

The crystal seemed to pulse with life against my palm. Elizabeth approached me cautiously.

27

"What just happened?" she asked.

She sipped her own glass of water with the baffled look of someone who had witnessed something she didn't have language to express.

I shrugged incredulously.

As for Coretta, Jocelyn said that during the session her daughter had moved her arm in a way she hadn't before but, other than that, there were no major changes to report. The few nurses and patients that had witnessed the session looked at us quizzically as we wheeled Coretta back to her room. Jocelyn continued to cry off-and-on, also somewhat speechless and overwhelmed by the whole ordeal.

Filled with a contagious spirit, Elizabeth and I visited a friend's home, determined to share our story and keep the evening alive. I told everyone about the energy that had taken hold of me, and how I'd begun to feel like I was fulfilling my destiny. I was aware that the spiritual presence I had embodied could be sensed by others. I felt it everywhere around me simply by remembering that it must have been there all along, only I'd been too blind to see it. Elizabeth was noticeably quiet, almost shivering. Her world had been upended too.

"It's like you're possessed," she said.

I stared back at her with penetrating eyes, my body coursing with electricity and my heart wide open. I wasn't even sure who or what *I* was anymore.

At about two in the morning, I went to the kitchen to make some tea. Upon glancing at the refrigerator, I was struck by a postcard stuck to the door. It was glossy purple and portrayed a caricature drawing of a young woman with long blonde curls and butterfly wings extending beyond either side of her back. The illustration was a near perfect match of Coretta. Beneath her in the drawing were a chain of drummers and dancers, all celebrating around a fire. I closed my eyes and recalled the night she and I had danced beside the fire in Belize. Then I remembered Bonnaroo, where we'd found each other in a timeless Tennessee wonderland.

Opening my eyes, I plucked the card from the fridge door and slowly turned it over. I gasped as I read the inscription: *Guardian Angel, Love and Protection.*

*   *   *

Upon returning to New York the following evening, I recounted the saga to my parents. They were skeptical, relegating such fairytales to movies and fantasy novels.

"What kind of drugs were you on?" asked my mother in a concerned and almost scornful tone. The skin around her eyes and forehead wrinkled like a prune.

My father remained silent, though I could tell my conviction made him nervous too.

Back at the law firm the next morning, I drank yerba maté and spent hours writing down my account of the experience, fully aware that my boss knew I was up to something. He didn't interrupt me, though, and when I had finished by mid-afternoon, I ran off several copies. I shared the story with a number of coworkers, many of whom already regarded me as strange, because I liked to talk about dreaming, yoga, and mysticism. Still, some of them took the time to read it and approached me in private so as to avoid prying eyes.

When my boss called me into his office, he sunk into a big leather chair behind his long, brown desk, still overflowing with piles of documents and dusty books. Through the clutter he saw that I had changed, and he asked me what was going on. I recounted my story, and he listened intently.

When I had finished, he remained silent for several moments, as if deciding how to respond. Finally, he spoke.

"You're wasting a gift by working here," he said. "Follow your heart. You can bring a lot of good to a lot of people."

I stayed on at the law firm throughout the winter, toiling away and saving as much money as I could. By March, when I could no longer stand the boredom and dissonance, I made up my mind to quit by the summer in order to begin traveling. One night in bed I imagined myself at a festival with camera in hand, just as I had envisioned a year earlier at the Sound Tribe concert. When I awoke I reached for my wallet and unfolded the scrap of paper on which I had scribbled my intentions so many months prior. The note seemed to vibrate, as if infused with an invisible life force, the seed of a dream waiting to germinate. Drifting back to sleep, I continued to dream about festivals and a few nights later—as I lingered on the edge of sleep—I visualized taking the portrait of a young woman donning costumed butterfly wings in a large, dusty field.

I hadn't seen Devon since the night before the healing session, but we spoke daily on the Lowdown and arranged to meet in New York in June. He'd been living check-to-check doing construction and, like me, had been looking for an excuse to break free and hit the road for good.

CHAPTER 4
BONNAROO

SIX MONTHS AFTER my defining moment at the hospital with Coretta, I left home without any firm plans to return. My parents, who had allowed me to stay with them throughout the previous year, didn't put up much resistance but were worried for my safety.

"It's your life," said my mother, needling me.

"Be careful, Son," added my father as he watched me pack my bags. "The world is a dangerous place."

Devon flew north to join me and together we sketched a rough itinerary. We would go "on tour" with Sound Tribe, following them to music festivals in upstate New York, Pennsylvania, Tennessee, Colorado and Northern California. Unbeknownst to me, Devon had also landed a temporary job at a salmon fishery in Alaska beginning mid-July, and suggested I meet him there once he had finished.

"Sure," I said.

After a muddy start at the Adirondack Mountain Music Festival, a few days respite in New York City, and a long weekend at the Creekside Jamboree in Pennsylvania, Devon and I drove through the night to Atlanta to reconnect with Penelope, who had graduated from college the previous month, exactly one year after us. She greeted us with warm hugs and chamomile tea, the early morning sunlight illuminating her thick, blond hair and jade green eyes. Even though our relationship had been tumultuous, she had been my first love and my heart fluttered every time I saw her.

"You boys look awful," she said. "Come inside and get cleaned up. Then you can cook me breakfast!"

While the two of them got reacquainted, gathered supplies and caught up on sleep, I shot over to Savannah to visit Coretta, who had emerged from her coma after seven difficult months. I spent two days with her and her family, evaluating her progress and taking long strolls along the oak-lined bluff with her and Jonathan, her boyfriend, who had stuck with her through everything.

She was confined to a wheelchair, couldn't speak, and had little-to-no short-term memory. Her face looked radically different on account of several reconstructive surgeries. She couldn't remember the accident nor anything that had happened after her sophomore year of college, including our semester together in Belize. She knew I was important to her, but she didn't know why. Using sign language, which she had learned as a child and had retained, she asked me to tell the story of how we'd met and repeatedly asked what had happened to her. Despite all this, I knew in my heart that somewhere inside her was the same intelligent, vibrant soul I'd fallen in love with. I also knew that any hope of a romantic relationship with her was lost.

On our last walk before I left for Atlanta, Jonathan and I wheeled Coretta along the bluff and began to talk about psychic phenomena, which was a shared interest between us.

Jonathan was lanky and baby-faced, with wise, hazel eyes and light brown hair that hung down over his forehead. He liked to kid Coretta by engaging her with abstract concepts she had once grasped easily but were now beyond her reach, or so we thought.

"What do you think about telepathy, Coretta? Do you think we can speak to each other with our minds?"

Her ears perked up. She clasped her turtle pendant in her left hand and raised her right hand. Using only her fingers, slowly spelled out, letter-by-letter:

I'm sending and receiving messages all the time.

Jonathan and I looked at each other in disbelief.

"Well, what do you know?" he said in his thick, Southern drawl. Placing his hand over the side of his mouth as if to shield Coretta, but speaking loudly enough for her to hear us, he leaned toward me and whispered, "She continues to amaze me, but it's going straight to her head."

Coretta let out a loud, belly laugh. "Can't help being smarter than you," she signed back.

Bidding farewell to Coretta and her family, I headed west to reconvene with Devon and Penelope. The following morning, we departed for Bonnaroo in separate cars, as Penelope wasn't sure where she was headed after the festival. By the time we crossed the Tennessee state line, traffic was at a stand-still. When we finally reached the gates after several sweaty hours spent crawling along the sizzling blacktop, we were ushered in opposite directions in order to find a campsite. Though we later discovered that we had landed practically within earshot of one another, I pitched my tent alone and set off on my own.

With camera in hand, I ventured out to explore the lay of the land. Bonnaroo was massive, even larger than the previous year. It was set on a mile-long stretch of farmland and designed to accommodate six stages with adjacent fields, numerous food courts and vending operations, hordes of pedestrian traffic, and abundant minivans, many of which had been converted into full-fledged mobile homes. Doing my best to conserve film, I found my way to a "shakedown" street—a parking lot marketplace, of which there were several, where attendees sold or traded their wares. Hippies were everywhere hawking homemade glass pipes, hemp necklaces, pot brownies and, occasionally, harder drugs. Here and there people stopped to chat as if everyone was an old friend.

It was in the midst of this crowd that I spotted the tall, exquisite, dark-haired woman I'd met the previous week in Pennsylvania. In fact, I had first noticed her months earlier at a steamy dance hall in Brooklyn. On that fateful night, the Antibalas Afrobeat Orchestra had been pumping out Fela Kuti covers and from my spot at the back of the club I could see her in the front row. By the time I had worked up the courage to talk to her, she had disappeared, and the opportunity had been lost.

In Pennsylvania, however, I had been busy taking photographs when, lo and behold, she'd approached me in search of an extra roll of film.

"Hey, photographer man!" she'd called out. "Any chance you can spare a roll?"

She had held up her orange, toy camera and flashed her large, brown, puppy-dog eyes and long lashes. I'd been amazed to see her standing before me. She had tied her hair in two long braids, and had worn a brightly-colored, knit tank-top and yellow, floral skirt.

My film costs $15 a roll, I'd thought to myself but did not say aloud, handing over two.

For my efforts, I had learned her name, Annabelle. She was a poet and barista from Staten Island.

"Hey, you're the guy with the funky pants!" she'd said.

Apparently, she had also recognized me from another festival the previous summer, where I'd worn bright orange pants I'd fashioned from an old dress. Eager to impress her, I had told her about the club in Brooklyn. Her giddy expression had shifted, and she'd instantly grown wary of my attention. While we'd shared space for a few dances, both aware of the other but not explicitly dancing together, the weekend had ended without our saying goodbye.

Imagine my surprise when I happened upon her amongst the masses at Bonnaroo five days later, along with another woman who appeared as eager for her affection as I was. Annabelle wore large sunglasses with dark lenses that covered half her face and the same knit, rainbow top. Her forearms were covered with thick, wooden bracelets and her fine black hair was once again tied in braids. When she sat cross-legged on the ground, I asked her if I could take her portrait and she reluctantly agreed. I could see her scrutinizing me from behind her black shades. We sat together for five minutes while she and her friend shared a cigarette, after which they abruptly stood, said "bye," and vanished into the crowd.

Later that night I found her again, alone this time, in the front row of the festival's opening concert put on by Antibalas—the same band from the club where I had first seen her. Aware that we were treading a similar path, we danced together and began to notice that our movements were almost uncannily identical and in synch.

"It's like we're of the same mold," I shouted over the noise as sweat poured down my face. She didn't hear me, but she smiled just the same.

The next morning, I sat near a stage drinking a cup of yerba maté and awaiting another Antibalas set when their manager, who was an old friend from high school, approached from behind and tapped me on the shoulder.

"I've got a present for you," he said, handing me a manila envelope, which I opened immediately.

"A backstage pass!" It was an all-access, golden ticket to the biggest party on the planet.

"It even covers your meals for the entire weekend," he said with pride.

"I can't believe it! Thank you! What can I do for you?"

"You can share your gift, and you can start by shooting my band."

I was whisked backstage into the artist tents and began eagerly taking candid photos of countless musicians prior to their performance. Moments later, I found myself on stage with Antibalas, moving with the music in an effort to capture the scene. I observed the crowd as an ebbing and flowing organism—all except Annabelle, who I spotted in the front row, beaming back at me.

As the day progressed I felt increasingly high despite not having taken any drugs. Brimming with confidence, I felt tuned-in to the rhythm of the festival and had no desire to sleep. I believed I was fulfilling my destiny and I didn't want to miss a minute of it. The all-encompassing, heartbeat-like *thump* of the bass resounded in every direction.

That evening I linked up with Devon and Penelope at the Sound Tribe show—their largest to date with over 10,000 people in attendance. After the show, I again ventured backstage in search of inspiration. It was there that I met Sound Tribe's guitarist, Hunter Brown. Somewhat star-struck, I tried to engage him by congratulating him on their packed house.

"Do you think you can be aware of the exact moment when your life changes forever?" I asked him.

"Aw, man," he said disappointedly, as if my silly attempt at conversation had broken his perfect concentration. "I believe anything is possible." With that he turned and walked away.

By Saturday night I began to feel touches of exhaustion but managed to maintain my wild pace by feeding off the atmosphere of a small dance tent overflowing with people. I could feel the energy of the crowd surging through my body as the DJ masterfully controlled the unseen intensity. Out of nowhere, Annabelle appeared. The moment we made eye contact, it started pouring. Relieved to have found each other once again, we danced together in the rain. Occasionally, we broke from our movement to embrace each other in long, soothing hugs that were filled with everything we had left in us. Emerging renewed again and again, we watched the sunrise over the farm as the rain transformed into a fine mist.

"Are you going to California for High Sierra?" I asked. The High Sierra Music Festival, held annually over the Fourth of July, was the next big stop on tour and less than a month away.

"Yes!" she said. "We'll find each other there."

Annabelle leaned in and tenderly kissed the center of my forehead. My body trembled. I thought of Coretta and imagined her looking back at me. She was smiling.

I felt a weight lift from my chest and tears streamed from my eyes. Annabelle held me against her until I stopped crying, then we ventured off in opposite directions, once again leaving it up to fate to bring us back together.

Meanwhile, back at the campsite, Devon was busy falling in love, too. He'd met a gentle, soft-spoken woman from Alabama named Aja, who had a small tattoo of half-a-butterfly on the outside of her left foot. I checked in with them and Penelope occasionally but, in their words, I was busy "playing rock star."

On the final afternoon of Bonnaroo, I was resting under a tree beside one of the dusty fields when I saw a radiant woman dressed as a sparkling butterfly, slowly weaving her way through the crowd. Possessed by a force beyond my control, I sprung to my feet to greet her and marveled at her whimsical beauty. Showering her with praise, I commented on the realization that—despite my own disbelief—she *was* the woman of the vision I'd had months earlier that had inspired me to quit my job. We shared an unearthly moment together as I photographed her and looked deep within her powder blue eyes. It was as if I had stepped into my own dream. Once she floated away, I had the unmistakable feeling I was on the right path.

Then, as the last rays of light cast long shadows across the festival, I noticed a narrow, dirt road leading to a part of the grounds I had yet to visit. It was as if a secret passageway had opened up. I heard Rob Newton's voice echo through my mind.

Don't be afraid to take the road less traveled.

It led to a balcony at the back, left corner of the main stage overlooking the entire concert field. A sea of nearly 100,000 people awaited the final performance of the weekend. It took several moments before I was able to fully conceive of such a thing. My mind felt like a balloon expanding to make room for the unfathomable sight.

Darkness descended over the farm as the Grateful Dead took the stage. It was exactly one year to the day since Coretta and I had found each other in that same field. On the anniversary, midway through the Dead's performance of "Sugar Magnolia," the same song that she and I had danced to, I spotted a giant balloon turtle surfing above the crowd. I didn't recognize it until it neared the foot of the stage and stalled in plain view, as if frozen within a window frame. My heart leapt at the synchronicity. I flashed back to Belize, where Coretta had first told me about her spiritual affinity for turtles. I remembered the pendant she wore around her neck, and how her home in Savannah was cluttered with images, dolls, and sculptures of turtles.

The bright green balloon drifted toward the front row. I felt Coretta's presence as if she were gripping me tightly around my chest and heard Rob's voice inaudibly emanating from the center of my head.

"Take it! Take it!" said the voice.

Strangely, it felt as if Devon and Coretta's boyfriend, Jonathan, who had also come to Bonnaroo and was somewhere in that crowd, were right there with me too. Pressing down on the shutter, I managed two or three exposures amidst the low light and rocking of the platform, but, as it was before the days of digital cameras, I had no idea whether I had gotten the shot.

After the show, I paced up and down the shakedown streets, as busy as city blocks, shooting photographs and sitting in on drum circles that rumbled steadily into the night. Still enchanted by my experience with the turtle, I wondered whether Coretta's spirit had really reached out to me, or if I had merely turned the coincidence into my own personal fantasy. Either way, Rob Newton was right. Reality *was* a little bigger than I thought, and we were just getting started.

CHAPTER 5
LADY

AFTER BONNAROO, Devon and Penelope headed West together while I made tracks across the country on my own. From Tennessee, I spent a night at a cheap motel in Oklahoma and another under the crystal clear, desert sky of New Mexico. Arriving well after dark, I imagined the parched, cracked earth teeming with sand-colored creepy-crawlers, rattlesnakes, scorpions and big, hairy spiders, all of them minding their own business. The air was dry and motionless except for the occasional howl of a coyote or screech owl. In the morning I packed up quickly and shifted north from Santa Fe toward Colorado. En route, I was greeted by torrential downpours. Riding high from the festival and relatively new to long road trips, I forged ahead without concern, even as my car began to hydroplane along slick stretches of I-25.

Minutes after the storm broke, I pulled over to watch a buffalo roam a lonely prairie. Once back on the road, I turned up the stereo, hit my stride, coasted over a hill, and promptly slid through another puddle. This time, I lost control of the steering wheel, slammed on the brakes and held my breath as the wheels locked and the car spun in a circle along the center of the interstate. Clutching the wheel so tightly that my fingernails dug into my palms, I wondered if I would die. After a complete three-sixty, the car skidded down into the median, snapped a steel road sign like a twig and abruptly came to rest in the grass. Exhaling deeply, my body shuddered involuntarily before melting into a pool of sweat.

The accident damaged the car's rear axle, but I walked away without a scratch. While awaiting a tow truck, I contemplated my sudden fall from grace and selfish illusion that I was somehow in control of everything. When the trucker arrived, I asked him to take me eighty miles north to Colorado Springs, the next closest town with its name in bold letters on my map. Instead, he persuaded me to have the car fixed in nearby Pueblo.

"It's a mechanic's town," he said reassuringly.

With my car in the shop indefinitely, the following afternoon I picked up a rental and drove to Denver, shrouded in rush hour traffic. Rather than getting tangled up, I cut west to Boulder in hopes of finding Elizabeth, who I had last seen during Coretta's healing session. I'd never been to Boulder and didn't know where she lived, so I made my way to a calm intersection before pulling over to call her.

"I'm in town," I said excitedly.

She was expecting me, but we hadn't confirmed a date for my arrival nor discussed the possibility of my staying with her.

"I'm on Arapahoe and Main," I said.

"Sounds like you're in the flow," she laughed. "I live right down the street."

"You're kidding?"

"Nope. Make a left and head straight to the end of the block. You're thirty seconds away."

43

Elizabeth was exactly as I remembered her: strong, confident, warm, grounding, and rooted in the present moment. As I emerged from the rental car she gave me a big hug.

"What happened?" she asked, inspecting the loaner.

"It's a long story."

"Well, you're here now. Want to take a walk?"

"There's nothing I'd rather do."

Grabbing a water bottle, she hopped into the passenger's seat and navigated us out of the neighborhood. Within minutes we were running up the side of a mountain in the Flatirons and watching the sunset above the city from the summit.

"You call that a walk?" I asked, gasping for air.

Elizabeth smiled and perched like an eagle. "Welcome to the Rockies," she said.

That evening, I met several of her friends. We ate a home-cooked meal and sang songs into the night. I was in awe of how quickly my fortune had turned. Life felt extraordinary again, as if balance had been restored.

I spent two laid back weeks at Elizabeth's awaiting a call about my car, which had remained on ice in Pueblo, a town full of mechanics though apparently lacking car parts. With the Fourth of July looming and my rendezvous with Annabelle in doubt, I grew anxious. The insurance money for the rental car had run out and my desire to forge ahead remained strong. Fortunately, Boulder was full of young people and beautiful parks, so I hiked daily and spent hours hanging out on the porch with Elizabeth's neighbors while she was at work.

Chelsea, who lived directly across the street, was also trying to find her way to California for High Sierra. One afternoon, as we brainstormed ways to catch a ride out West, I glanced down at her bare left foot and noticed a tattoo of a half-butterfly. It was identical to the one that Devon's new love interest, Aja, wore on her foot.

"Where did you get that tattoo?" I inquired.

"In Alabama, where I grew up. My best friend has the other half."

I was shocked.

"Is your best friend Aja?" I said.

"Yes!"

"I just met her at Bonnaroo! My buddy Devon is in love with her! What are the chances of that?"

Chelsea perked up.

"Wow," she said, though she didn't seem as mystified as I was.

"I don't know what to make of all these synchronicities," I said.

"That kind of stuff happens when you're on the road. It's the Divine showing you you're on the right path."

Talking about the Divine still made me uncomfortable. To me, it was just another way of saying "God."

"Have you tried asking it for help?" she said.

"Help with what?" I shrugged.

"With anything. You'd be surprised how often it'll answer you. Try it out. Ask for a ride to California."

"I've got to go," I said, and dashed off to check my email.

With my head still spinning from this latest coincidence, I wandered into an internet café and signed onto the Lowdown, posting a message on the ride-share board. Within minutes, I received a reply. A woman offering me a ride would be passing through town at sundown, about thirty-six hours prior to the start of the festival. Looking at a map, I calculated that Boulder was at least twenty-two hours away, separated by the rolling hills of Wyoming, the salt flats of Utah, the barren Nevada desert and, finally, the sprawling High Sierra, for which the festival was named.

My ride, a grandiose, weathered behemoth of a van, pulled up at twilight as the sky turned lavender and the mosquitoes emerged for their evening feast. My benefactors were a couple of seasoned nomads: a short, stout girl named D., ("Just D.," she said upon introducing herself) and Lady, a corpulent, sharp-mouthed wayfarer from Amarillo, Texas. She may have been the most physically imposing person I had ever met. Her van had survived the late 70s. It was suntan brown with an orange racing-stripe jetting across the sliding door. Its charred tires were nearly stripped to the bone and revealed every wrinkle of the vehicle's "one thousand festivals, one million miles," as Lady put it. I tossed my backpack inside and climbed into the monstrosity of a mobile home, carving out a clutter-free space the size of a milk crate before bidding farewell to Elizabeth. She read my nervous expression.

"If you never expect anything, you'll never be disappointed," she said, before bowing her head as we drove away.

Leaning into my portable, foam camping chair, in its last days from extended use, I examined the innards of this ludicrous, mechanical camel as it swayed to and fro, struggling to grip the center of the road. The back half of the van housed a mattress and served as an all-purpose living space, closet and hamper. It smelled of week-old laundry but seemed cozy enough under the circumstances.

"If you ever want me to drive, just give a holler," I called out to Lady over the deafening *whirr* of the muffler.

"This here's my home and don't you forget it, dude," she boomed from the driver's seat.

As she leaned back from the steering wheel her chair shifted abruptly, letting out a loud *screech*. It was like a scene out of a cartoon.

"Jesus, I'm totally pre-menstrual!" she added, "so don't give me any lip either. I'll drop you off right here to *die* if I have to!"

She popped two aspirin and took a giant slug from her super-sized thermos full of iced green tea mixed with yerba maté. I couldn't get over the sheer scale of her. Without question, this was her ship and she meant every word of her threats.

The van's side panels were covered in beige insulation with patches of exposed steel. We pushed through the barren Wyoming night. The moonlight struggled through the distressed cloth curtains muting the back portholes and casting an iridescent glow across the protruding metal foundation of a chair that had been torn out of the floor. A rusty, jagged beam

47

rested between my knees, mere inches from my groin. I leaned against the cold metallic wall, nerve-racked with vibration, and tried to sleep but didn't catch a single wink. D. rode shotgun, oblivious it seemed, in a chair that also shifted violently from side to side with the slightest movements of the hull. From the looks of it, the seatbelt had perished long ago.

"I've never made it through Utah without some kind of problem," announced Lady while at a truck stop around 3 a.m.

What have I gotten myself into, I thought.

As the first specks of daylight caressed the golden, plastic dashboard covered in crystals and other relics of the vessel's ancient past, our semi-conscious torpor ended abruptly. A loud *pop!* jarred us awake. The left rear tire had exploded along a barren stretch of I-80. The back of the van slumped to the ground like a wounded animal. D., who had taken the wheel in Salt Lake City, began screaming hysterically, further rupturing the sleeping giant's brief rest. In that instant, however, Lady struck me as the type of woman who always slept with one eye open.

Auspiciously, the van's well-distributed girth prevented any serious loss of control and D. managed to work it to the curb. We spilled out onto the empty highway to collect ourselves. Lady immediately dialed her mother in Amarillo, unloading all her frustration over the phone.

"This is all your fault, Mom! I'm out here in the middle of nowhere with my friends and the bloody van blew a tire! You were supposed to get those tires changed!"

"It's your van, sweetheart," said the crackling voice on the other end of the line. "*You* were supposed to get them changed."

"Mom! I can't deal with this right now. I'm totally pre-menstrual. Just call a tow truck for us, will ya?"

"Ok," relented the sleepy voice.

After hanging up, Lady took a deep breath, settled down and found solace in her crystal collection, which she stored in a black, plastic hard-case with gray foam lining.

Meanwhile, D. was distraught and unable to pull herself together. She'd panicked upon exiting the van and had accidentally knocked her favorite piece of topaz onto the unforgiving pavement, where the crystal broke in half.

"Such a bad omen," she mumbled to herself as she tried in vain to fit the pieces together.

Madness, I thought. *Sheer madness.*

I looked at the clock on the dashboard. It was 5:30 a.m. and everything was falling apart, yet I felt invigorated and totally at peace with the world. I was once again completely out of control and stranded on the highway, but in perfect health and gazing out at a marvelous sunrise over the vast, twinkling white salt flats. Without hesitation, I grabbed my camera and began snapping photographs. The dream-like quality of the landscape seemed to invite me in. Locking eyes with Lady for the first time since we'd met, we shared a moment of understanding, even a smile, as she nestled in the ragged comforters of her home and placated herself with her precious stones.

"You're alright," she said to me. "I'm glad you're here and not somebody else."

By mid-afternoon we had a new tire, were back on the road and things were looking up. But, no sooner were we mobile than Lady's dark cynicism and forked tongue returned to permeate the thick, musty air of the van. After swinging through Reno to pick up the best burritos I had ever tasted, we finally crossed over into California where the emerald green tree line of the Sierras welcomed us like Shangri-La.

I was exiled to the far rear of the van after Lady verbally assaulted me for not having offered to drive—*poor memory*, I assumed—for never having driven a van that size and, subsequently, for my unfamiliarity with the way it handled. Back at the wheel, her rage slightly diffused after popping some Valium, she proceeded to guide us deeper into the mountains. I sat silently, slowly roasting as the van became a blazing hot oven beneath the implacable sun.

Lady missed the turn-off to the festival grounds on two consecutive passes. Despite the delays, we were still a day early and eventually settled into a small cottage for the night, some ten miles north of our destination. Sitting on the front porch looking out at the stars, D. and I commented on the nearly inescapable chaos that seemed to precede every festival. Our rollercoaster ride appeared to have come to an end. Sadly, we were mistaken.

CHAPTER 6
CUCKOO

AS WE APPROACHED THE GATES to High Sierra,
tensions rose yet again as Lady began to dictate where we
would camp once inside. Instead of making a scene, the instant
we parked I scooped up my backpack and headed away as fast
as I could. Lady seemed unconcerned by my departure; she was
too busy ordering the others around. I felt a weight lift with
each step I took, and I was proud that I had squelched the fire
blazing within me rather than blowing up at her.

Within a minute I bumped into two friends from the
Lowdown that I had met on tour. They led me to a new
campsite under a tall ponderosa pine. I started to pitch my tent
there, only to halt at the sight of Penelope, who appeared out of
the blue and invited me to camp with her, Devon and some
mutual friends who had made the trip. My heart leapt when I
saw them as it felt like I'd returned home where I belonged.

It wasn't long before somebody broke out the psychedelics
and everyone began tripping on one substance or another. I
leaned over to Penelope, who was lying on the ground looking
up at the sky.

"So, this is what they do in California?" I joked.

"You ain't seen nothin' yet," she said.

Having ingested a few wrinkled, brown, psilocybin
mushrooms, Devon, Penelope and I headed out for a walk with

our cameras. As the 'shrooms kicked in, I became acutely aware of my heightened senses. Upon entering the main concert field, we sat down in the warm, green grass. I looked over at Penelope. To my amazement, she was surrounded by a distinctive purple glow that illuminated a large, circular area of space extending beyond her roughly ten feet in every direction.

"I think I can see your aura," I said.

"Neat!" she said.

Curious if I could capture the ethereal hue, I attempted to photograph her but as I pressed down on the shutter, the camera's battery died. I was convinced that her energy field had blown it out. Sitting beside her was like sticking a finger in a wall socket—she was electric.

Stowing my camera in my hip pack, Devon and I continued on toward the other end of the festival grounds while Penelope wandered off on her own. We stopped about five feet from the edge of a performance tent and Devon lit up a hand-rolled cigarette. Suddenly, I perceived an unearthly ripple that fractured the simple rhythm of our surroundings. It was similar to a sound but shockingly more visceral and vivid, as if it existed beyond ordinary reality. A quick *shu-shu-shu-shu-shu*, it sounded like a torch being dragged through the air, or the beating wings of a small bird flying right past your ears. Simultaneously, my vision involuntarily rotated one hundred-eighty degrees with blazing speed—faster than my physical body could possibly have turned. For the slightest instant, I had eyes in the back of my head, literally! I caught sight of two shimmering silver flashes of light emanating from either side of a beautiful, young woman. The incident took my breath away.

The young woman quickly crossed her arms over her chest and hunched over in embarrassment, as if she'd been caught naked. Peeking up at me, she flashed an enormous smile, giggled and blushed furiously, then ran off haphazardly before burying her head in the arms of a young man with a long, dark beard whose face I couldn't see.

"Did you see that!?" I asked Devon.

"See what?"

When I turned back around to find her, she'd vanished. I promptly relayed my experience to Devon and, while he believed me, he shrugged his shoulders and was at a loss for words.

Devon promptly ran back to camp to find some of whatever I had taken. Thoroughly enchanted, I ventured inside the performance tent and sat alone, cross-legged on the ground, as the next concert began. One by one, members of the Sun Ra Arkestra floated through the small audience en route to the stage. Each member wore an elaborate robe and colorful turban, and together they looked like a troupe of desert-dwelling, intergalactic, afrofuturistic monks. There were roughly ten of them and as they walked they chanted in unison: "Space is the place… Space is the place."

My mind scrambled for a foothold, flipping through a series of vivid images before settling on the memory of the beautiful silver light. As the vision filled my awareness, it felt as if a hidden chamber in the center of my chest unlocked, and

53

my whole being was flooded with ecstasy. Radiance ignited and beamed forth from my heart, and a ridiculous smile spread across the width of my face. I felt like I was enormous, glowing, and sharing this unique and wondrous feeling with everyone else in the tent. *Space is the place,* I thought. *Space is the place.*

The following evening, Devon introduced me to an older, gray-haired man who called himself "Cuckoo." Devon had met him the previous night after we'd all split up. Cuckoo immediately struck me as a classic, crazy hippy for whom the '60's had never ended.

"I'm just an old guy, been to a lot of Dead shows," he mumbled, but his cavernous brown eyes, bordering on black, and devilish smile were giveaways. There was more to him than he let on. We spent several hours listening to his stories from the road, laughing uncomfortably at his dirty jokes. I tried to enjoy his company, but as the night wore on I grew increasingly wary of him. The longer we sat, the drowsier I became. My mind started to feel like scrambled eggs, and I felt as if my energy was being drained. Beyond that, Cuckoo seemed to be passively leading us on some kind of telepathic journey. I found myself acting as if my will wasn't my own and was convinced that he could read my thoughts. Afraid, I withdrew and grew silent, which provoked animosity from him.

"Why are you hiding?" he asked. "You can trust me. I'm just an old guy."

I looked over at Devon, hoping he would align with me, but his glassy stare told me he had already committed to Cuckoo for the evening.

"Are you coming to see Sound Tribe?" I asked.

"Nah," said Devon. I'm going to hang with Cuckoo."

"Suit yourself. I'll see you later."

Gripped by loneliness and left to wonder about my issues with trust and judgment, I headed off through the woods toward the late-night music hall. Along the way I stumbled upon a "freak parade" led by a pogo-legged, goat-man painted white with long, curly horns and white accordion-tube scarves wrapped around his skin-tight bodysuit. Giant metallic springs on either leg allowed him to lap even the fleetest of pedestrians, each of whom he soaked with a water cannon full of unpleasant, lukewarm liquid.

"I ran out of water so I filled it with LSD!" he shouted over the sound of people fleeing.

"Is everybody here out of their mind?" I yelled back.

"I'm just kidding, man. I'd be crazy to waste that much LSD… or would I? Hahahahaha!" laughed the goat-man as he hopped away.

Emerging from the onslaught, I arrived at the hall where Sound Tribe had begun a four-hour musical journey through the night. As I stepped inside, my skin began to crawl. It dawned on me that everyone in the room was on psychedelics. The band was in the groove, like interstellar shamans powering a spaceship through the cosmos. I felt that I could communicate telepathically with everybody there, and that we were enjoying some sort of mystical party as we tuned-in to the same frequency. The sense of separation between us melted away and, at one point, it seemed as if I was able to access the entire universe with my mind. Closing my eyes, I saw my father as if he were right there in front of me.

"You're always with me, aren't you, Dad?" I said.

"You bet I am," he replied. "I love you, Son."

I started to cry. "I love you too, Dad!

"Be careful out there," he said. "Things aren't always what they appear to be."

Penelope, dressed in a flowing, bright blue jumpsuit and platform shoes, emerged from the crowd and planted herself inches away from me. After all we'd been through, she was like family and I was overjoyed to see her. We stood perfectly still beside one another and I could feel a subtle vibration run up my spine as waves of energy passed between us. Unsure as to whether she was feeling it too, I closed my eyes and concentrated on the center of my forehead, which almost immediately produced a tingling sensation in my palms.

"Whoa! That's what I'm talking about!" she yelped, her body swooning as if she'd been shocked. I smiled back, pleased that my body seemed to know what to do even though my mind had no clue what was going on.

After the show we returned to our campsite, where I lied down for a short nap. To my dismay, I awoke the following afternoon to the sounds of people slowly crawling into their cars and making for the exit. As I hadn't found Annabelle, who I had hoped to travel with, I'd made tentative plans to catch a ride north to the Oregon Country Fair with a neighboring camper. I had heard that the Fair, held each July just outside Eugene, was full of faerie-folk and would be a photographer's paradise but, unbeknownst to me, my neighbor had disappeared as clandestinely as she'd arrived. For a moment, I panicked. I was miles from nowhere and without transportation. Luckily, Devon and Penelope had made plans to head to San Francisco with another new friend, Tristan, a good-looking, free-spirited yoga instructor and rare gem collector. It didn't take much convincing to hop on the bandwagon, although I had to ride with Cuckoo, who lived in Berkeley, since both Penelope's and Tristan's cars were packed to the gills. I reluctantly agreed.

In the moments prior to leaving, a particularly slender, grotesque, middle-aged man wandered upon our campsite and struck up a conversation with me. He called himself Lane in the Rain, and also invited me to San Francisco to stay with him, though I politely declined and continued to pack my bag. When I turned back to wish him well, I found a lone peacock feather resting in his place.

"A protective eye," said Penelope, who had witnessed the interaction and knew I didn't trust Cuckoo.

As I stowed the last of our bags in the caravan, I handed Devon my cell phone as he still didn't have one, and Cuckoo had offered to let me use his in case of emergency. I climbed into Cuckoo's van, attempting to embrace the opportunity to face my fears and intending to thank him for the lessons he had inadvertently taught me about trust a few nights earlier. It wasn't long, however, before his reckless driving put me on

57

edge. I shot him a disapproving glance to let him know I was unimpressed.

"Humans can't take me out," he said arrogantly as he hit the gas and veered sharply around a line of cars. Moments later he stopped short, backtracked a few hundred yards and jumped out to salvage a tattered pair of pants and equally rotten pair of shoes that had been discarded along the roadside. I shielded my eyes from him.

"What?" he barked. "This stuff's still good."

Unnerved, I wondered about his motives and questioned what little I had learned of him since we'd met. As we continued on, my negative thoughts got the best of me and I started to panic once again. I was alone with a stranger and without my phone. On top of that, I didn't have a map nor any clue where we were. Cuckoo picked up on my anxiety and immediately lit a huge joint, took a long drag and passed it to me. I foolishly took two hits before my vision began to blur. Cuckoo's voice softened, his words becoming more careful and crafted.

"We're just on a path," he whispered. "That's all it is. Just follow your path. Fate brought us together."

As he spoke I could feel my self-control slipping away, replaced by a numbing fog. He was mesmerizing me.

"Hey, why don't we go to my cabin in Sonoma?" he said. "That's a great idea, right?"

I could feel his words attacking my will, and my solar plexus contracted painfully. He reached for his phone and placed a call. Suddenly, my body shivered from head to toe and my mind exploded with visions of rape and torture that intensified as he spoke to a friend.

"I might have found what we talked about," he said excitedly to whoever was on the other end of the line.

Shaking furiously and in a cold sweat, as a last resort I harnessed all my strength and sent a prayer to my friends, silently screaming the words, *please help!* A few seconds later, I felt a quick jolt of electricity shoot through my left hand, which I imagined to be some sort of acknowledgment. Cuckoo must have felt it too as he let out an odd, uncomfortable laugh and looked at me maliciously.

A couple minutes passed before he placed another phone call, this time to a woman. I could hear her howling at him frantically from the other end of the line.

"Damn! We're out of gas," he interrupted. "Hang on a sec, would ya?"

We came to a halt at a dusty fill station alongside the main road. To my amazement, Tristan pulled in right behind us, witnessing the tail end of Cuckoo's heated argument over the phone with a woman he claimed was his girlfriend.

"What kind of crazy trip are you on?" yelled the woman's voice through the speaker, loud enough to cut through the sound of whirring engines. Without hesitation I grabbed my backpack, climbed into a crawlspace in the back of Tristan's car and instantaneously began to calm down.

"What happened?" asked Devon, confused.

"I don't know, but I feel one-hundred percent better now that I'm here with you." I let out a huge sigh of relief.

"Where are you going?" said Cuckoo. "You're gonna leave me to ride alone?"

I bit my lip and looked away.

"What about your friend, the other guy?" He motioned for Devon to keep him company in exchange for me.

"I'm good, thanks," said Devon, suddenly enlightened as to Cuckoo's insidious motives.

"What about some gas money?" pleaded Cuckoo.

"Sorry man, gotta jet," said Tristan as he hopped into the driver's seat. Locking the doors, he hit the gas, off we rode, and that was the last we saw of Cuckoo.

CHAPTER 7
THE DELICATE ARCH

IN SAN FRANCISCO, Devon, Penelope and I slept on the floor of an unfurnished penthouse apartment near Chinatown that Tristan was watching for a friend. Then, we rode with him back to Colorado, pausing briefly in Reno for burritos and to visit a gem shop.

We decided to break in Moab. The thermometer read one hundred-ten degrees Fahrenheit in the shade. Penelope suggested that we fast for a day to detoxify our bodies. Despite not eating, we all felt strong after consuming fourteen ounces of fruit juice and a few liters of water to withstand the merciless sun.

At the edge of town, a gas station attendant suggested we stay for the sunset at Arches National Park. In particular, she recommended hiking to the Delicate Arch, a famous monument located high on a cliffside. Upon viewing the majestic arch from a lookout far below, I was inspired to trek the mile-and-a-half up the mountain to experience it up close. It was as if the wind of the place was calling me. Devon, Penelope and Tristan decided they wanted to enjoy the sunset at the Windows, a series of cave-like formations on the opposite end of the park and much lower to the ground.

Prior to splitting up, we each drank a small portion of the mushroom tea we had brought from California.

"You take the rest," said Tristan, winking. He handed me what remained of it in a small water bottle.

As we separated, Penelope placed her favorite piece of smoky quartz crystal in my palm. I had found that holding the crystal incited pleasant sensations in my body and had hoped to take it with me but hadn't asked her for it.

"You read my mind," I said appreciatively.

"Maybe you read mine," she said.

The beginning of the hike took me along a vast, deserted slope of red rock. I wove across the mountain slowly in an effort to realize its entirety. Occasionally, I'd stop to sip the tea until I felt that my stomach couldn't handle any more, though at no point did I feel disoriented or "on drugs." If anything, I felt incredibly clear-headed and energized. As I walked I came across three hikers about my age, two women and a man, who I had first noticed upon setting out. They were resting on a small boulder, and I felt drawn to them though I didn't know why. One of the women was bright red in the face and looked ill and as I passed, I had the sudden urge to turn back to help her. I had been clutching the smoky quartz as I'd walked but handed it to her without any rationale.

"Here, hold this," I said. "Hopefully it will help."

As she cradled the crystal in her hands, I spontaneously focused on sending her healing energy. After a minute she said she felt a little better and returned the stone. When I touched it, it produced a sharp jolt of electricity that shot up my left arm.

Continuing toward the arch, I noticed that the three hikers seemed to trace my footsteps for a short time. Soon I was alone again, slightly removed from the handful of other hikers pacing up and down the poorly established path. Next, I followed a trail marked by stones through a narrow, cavernous gully that snaked along the outside of the mountain and up into a three-foot wide path that hugged the rock wall. To the left of the path was a cliff with a straight drop hundreds of feet to the valley floor. A warm breeze swept up the cliffside and brushed against my sweaty skin like a wave.

When I reached the last stretch, a slender conduit pressed against the north face of the mountain, I spotted a small, triangular arch situated ten feet above my head in the rock wall. I found it interesting but didn't stop to examine it. Instead, I continued around the bend to the much larger, Delicate Arch some fifty yards away. Named for its improbable, gravity-defying shape, the Delicate Arch was on the opposite side of a crimson-colored, rock bowl that swirled down and behind the remarkable formation. A vulture glided by overhead, as if superimposed over the palpable, powder blue sky.

Many people lined the edge of the bowl surrounding the arch, murmuring and snacking as they watched the day's last light cast a pinkish glow across the rocks. Rather than mingle with the tourists, I decided to sneak down behind the arch to view the sunset through it. I settled on a small ledge where I could rest out of sight. As I relaxed to wait for dusk, I became preoccupied with finding a "power spot" in order to capture the energy of the place, a notion I'd garnered from Carlos Castaneda's books on shamanism.

After a few moments of focused breathing to calm my nerves and awaken my senses, I felt an unexpected shift in consciousness, as if I had entered into a dream. The colors around me were brighter, objects appeared somewhat hazy and ephemeral, my skin felt transparent, and my hearing was piqued. It was then that I had a clear, life-like vision of an unfamiliar, elderly man with a long, gray beard. I was further shocked when the image of this stranger both visually and "audibly"—via a resounding, silent voice within my mind— suggested that I descend further down the mountain behind the arch and around a clearly defined bend leading to the endless chasm below. I shivered with fear.

I tried to deny the urge to explore but my curiosity won out. The centers of my palms began to heat up and tingle as I removed my rubber sandals, hooked them to my hip pack, and set off barefoot down the steep southern face, carefully tiptoeing in a long switchback pattern to maintain balance. Soon, I reached a sharp ledge. Pausing there, I realized that I might not be able to ascend again should I decide to cross the treacherous threshold. Taking another deep breath, I slid further down.

Suddenly, I stumbled. My body froze. I heard the haunting echo of a loosened stone cascading down the endless rock wall. Gathering my courage and securing my footing, I progressed along the edge of the wall in an effort to turn the corner. After a few more paces I came to a large, flat rock that must have fallen from far above as it was the only one of its kind. My eyes opened wide to the vista of the awe-inspiring canyon below. I knew this was the place I'd been seeking.

Stashing my camera in my pack, I gazed out at the western skyline, flooded with soft clouds and a pleasant lavender hue. Spotting the smaller, triangular arch I had passed near the end of the trail, I marveled at the way it framed the setting sun like a tiny window ablaze with orange light. Unlike my previous attempts at meditation, this time I kept my eyes wide open and remained focused on the window as I attempted to still my whirling mind. Within a few moments, it seemed as if the spectacular vista around me was dissolving. I strained not to blink, determined to catch a glimpse of what Castaneda described as "the crack between the worlds." Gradually, all that remained in my field of vision was the small arch and the pyramid of orange light that shown through it, now amplified between my eyes. It was as if I could reach out to touch it.

As my meditation deepened, I perceived a number of feminine presences offering me yoga postures as if they were instructions. My body seemed to shift involuntarily and I completely lost touch with my exact position, although I remained very much aware of the sheer magnitude of the surroundings. At one point, I even desired to merge with it by giving myself to the spectacular gorge, but I decided that it wasn't the right time and that the connections with my loved ones were too important to surrender. I didn't feel depressed at the thought of jumping. Rather, I was consumed with immense joy and an indelible sense of interconnectedness with everything.

After half-an-hour, I heard the silent voices of my friends calling out to me as if they were right beside me. Gathering my belongings, I scrambled back up the cliffside. About halfway up I came to the threshold—the ledge too steep to climb, too smooth to grip, and too tall to leap over. I cowered. I hesitated, scanning the rock for the safest route of ascent and doing my best to avoid looking down at the ominous chasm below. In that moment, fear *was* the mountain—the two were inseparable. My ears started ringing, my blood was boiling, and Death pressed down against my shoulders.

Taking an enormous gulp of air, I held my breath and hurled myself vertically against the rock, abandoning any foot support beneath me and hugging the ancient stone wall for dear life. Not wasting any time, with my next move I summoned every ounce of strength I had and thrust myself upward onto a safer platform.

I sighed with relief and my body flooded with endorphins. I felt like I had conquered a demon. A cleansing ecstasy ensued.

Climbing up from behind the Delicate Arch to the befuddlement of the few lingering tourists who saw me, I inspected the scene before gazing once more at the small, triangular arch in the distance. The window within the arch was still gleaming with orange light, though now it framed the silhouette of three people. Somehow, I knew they were the three hikers I had encountered upon my initial ascent. When I fixed my attention on them, I immediately felt as if we were locked-in, engaging in some sort of telepathic and energetic exchange. My eyes closed. I perceived silver lights shooting through my arms as they involuntarily swung downward, crisscrossed in front of my waist, then rose upward and outward alongside my body and overhead, like flapping wings. A flood of rainbow lights emanated from my midsection outward in all directions. I sensed the extreme power of an unseen force, as if I was releasing a cache of energy I'd stored at the rock. I performed these motions as if someone was moving me like a puppet, before I heard a woman's silent voice.

"Stop it! You'll hurt him!" said the voice.

In an instant, the ethereal light disappeared. I felt as if a tractor beam between us had been broken. I hunched over in agony, my abdomen burning.

Thoroughly confounded, I peered curiously around the dark, abandoned red rock bowl before heading back down the mountain. Devon, Penelope and Tristan were waiting for me at the foot of the trail. We hugged and stretched for a few moments in preparation for the last leg of our journey, an overnight haul to Boulder.

"What happened?" asked Devon. "There's something different about you." Penelope leaned in, eavesdropping.

"It was incredible," I said, "but I'd rather not talk about it now. How about you?"

"Amazing. As the sun set I held Penelope in my arms and I could see every bone in her body. I had x-ray vision!"

"Wow. How do we explain this stuff?" I said.

"The real question is, will anyone believe you?" said Penelope.

"I think it's evolution," said Devon.

Tristan wandered over to us, grinning as if he had orchestrated the whole thing.

"Time to move on," he said.

"Just one more minute, ok?" I said.

Turning to face the north, I leaned over into a forward bend, holding it for a few long breaths. Devon stood beside me, five feet to my right, mimicking my movements. As I lifted up and out of the posture, I raised my arms alongside my torso in the same flapping motion I'd performed involuntarily upon leaving the Delicate Arch. Once again, I saw rainbow lights emanating from my midsection. This time, I felt pressure as if I were pushing up through a tank of water, which caused me to exhale strongly. The combination produced a surreal *shu-shu-shu-shu-shu* sound, identical to the one I had heard a week earlier at High Sierra in California. Simultaneously, Devon let out a peculiar groan and hit the ground with a *thud*, snapping me out of my ethereal vision. His body convulsed for two or three seconds before he quickly sat up and brought his hand to his mouth.

"I think I broke my tooth," he said in a daze.

"You had a seizure!" shrieked Penelope, who rushed to his aid and applied a cloth to his lower lip, which was streaming blood.

"I guess I did. I'm okay though. Actually, I feel great, except for my mouth. I don't know what happened. All I remember is that I was stretching and saw these beautiful lights passing through my belly."

"Shockwave," said Tristan, who had patiently observed the whole scene from his seat on the hood of his car. "I felt it all the way over here."

On the way out of town we stopped for gas and got Devon some ice for his wounds, then rode off into the night toward Colorado. A lightning storm brewed beyond the confines of the car as I dangled my hands out the window to soak up the wind through my palms, still tingling. Gradually, my eyes closed and the purple desert skyline faded away. I felt deep gratitude for my traveling companions, trusting them as I would my family. Still, as the heaviness of sleep swept over me, I couldn't help but wonder what sort of strange magic we had unearthed.

CHAPTER 8
COLORADO

WE TOUCHED DOWN SAFELY in Boulder, and Devon found a dentist to repair his broken tooth. Then, he departed for Alaska. Tristan, in search of further adventures, took off on his own toward points unknown. Meanwhile, Penelope and I caught up on weeks of missed sleep and ambled around town.

One evening at dusk we were engrossed in conversation about whether there's such a thing as "old souls." While we talked, she led me down a hill to a small house on the corner. An immaculate flower garden filled the front yard. Inside the gate stood an elderly, gray-bearded man in his mid-seventies, diligently tending to his plants with an old, tin watering can. When he saw us, he beckoned us into his hideaway and gave us a tour. We appreciated the delightful array of colors and scents for several minutes. It appeared that each flower had been placed in such a fashion so as to accentuate the features of the next and to elevate the sensory experience of the admirer.

While we perused the garden, our host, William, began to share with us the details of his work in UFO studies, parapsychology and psychic phenomena.

"That's what brought you here, isn't it, a couple of old souls like you?" he said.

Penelope and I looked at each other.

"I'm a master of ESP," he announced proudly, "and a scholar of astrology."

Offering us some chairs, he brought out iced tea and began to tell us a story of a college professor who had impressed upon him the power of understanding astrology and its relation to human nature.

"This science is still very much alive and well in India," said William. "The stars can tell you where you've been, where you are, and where you're going. Not just in this life, mind you, but over the course of many lives."

I instantly regarded William as one of the most engaging people I had ever met, and his direct gaze into my eyes sent waves of soothing vibrations from the center of my skull down to my toes. I could tell Penelope was feeling these waves of energy too by the way her body slackened when he addressed her. It was evident that William was more interested in her than me, and I quietly started to brood. Gradually, he turned toward me with such intensity that the crickets stopped chirping.

"Laugh, and the world laughs with you," he said. "Cry, and you'll weep in your beer." I did my best to feign a smile.

When we left his home it suddenly dawned on me that the face I had visualized at the Delicate Arch—that of an elderly man with a long, gray beard—and the silent voice that had coaxed me down the mountain was William's. The similarities were striking, but the synchronicity was difficult to fathom. Determined to gain some answers and aware that my time in Colorado was nearing an end, the following evening I visited

William again on my own. He greeted me warmly, and I told him about my vision.

"Not uncommon," he said matter-of-factly. "Why don't you come in for some tea?"

He sat me down in a small library overflowing with books and began to speak about the "Universal Mind."

"The Universe is a receptive, giving, self-conscious organism capable of interacting with us and guiding our lives toward a higher purpose," he said.

I hung onto every word.

"When I was a young man about your age," he continued, "I was hitchhiking across Wyoming in a delivery truck when we were thrown off the road during a thunderstorm. I fell out of the truck and was badly injured. My eyes were full of blood and I couldn't see. I thought I might die. I'd nearly given up when an unearthly female voice guided me to safety. She instructed me on how to properly bandage myself and commanded me to leave the driver, whom she assured me was in stable condition. Then, she revealed to me a path to the road by teaching me to focus my 'third eye' antenna on the spot, like a laser. As I stumbled along, she blasted me with 'white lightning' on the top of my head—my crown *chakra*—although I didn't know about chakras at the time. 'You have a choice,' she said. 'Remain awake and live, or die now, ascend, and view a sight of the change you would have affected in the world had you lived.'"

William paused there as if to tighten the reins. I was transfixed, almost paralyzed, yet ready to jump out of my seat with excitement.

"Obviously, I chose life," he said after an interminable moment, giggling a bit as he'd sensed my predicament. "And I've lived each day as an offering ever since."

"Wow! What a story!" Finally exhaling, I sunk back down in the chair.

"Yeah, wow," he said, nostalgic.

Following his tale, William imparted knowledge of outer realms, other dimensions and invisible, "clinging spirits" that often live among us, and shared wisdom garnered from various psychic encounters he'd had throughout his lifetime. Riveted by his lucid delivery and utterly believable manner of speaking, my entire body experienced an overwhelming vibration that increased the more sincerely I listened.

"My advice to you, my young friend, is to never stop learning. And, if you're curious, repeat this mantra from time to time. Are you ready?"

I nodded.

"I wish to be an instrument of the Universe, filled with infinite love and infinite wisdom."

I repeated the words back to him. "I wish to be an instrument of the Universe, filled with infinite love and infinite wisdom."

He beamed back at me proudly. "You see, the Universe perfects its instruments…"

I left William's home after three unforgettable hours, feeling as if I had just received an indefinable gift.

The next morning, the mechanic in Pueblo called to inform me that my car was finally ready, exactly thirty days after I'd abandoned it. I could feel the tides turning and things started moving quickly. I said goodbye to Elizabeth, dropped Penelope off at the airport, and immediately headed south. During the two-hour drive I began to notice a strange vibration in my lips and a boost in my sensitivity. I felt like I was "activated" again—similar to how I had felt when I'd first visited Coretta in the hospital.

After retrieving my car, I had the sudden urge to call Devon, who I was planning to meet in Alaska two weeks later. Rather than wasting cell phone minutes, I stopped at a local bank to use their landline instead. As I lifted the handset, my cell phone rang anyway. It was Devon.

"That's crazy. I was just dialing you," I said.

"Right," he answered, and then paused, as if to convey that his timing was perfectly natural.

I filled him in on my whereabouts and all that had happened since he'd left Boulder, including my enlightening conversation with William.

"I'm heading your way right now," I said.

"Good. Hurry! I've been packing fish nonstop. It smells awful!" he laughed. "Be safe out there, man. See you in a couple weeks."

A bank worker sitting at the desk beside me overheard the conversation. After I'd hung up, she turned to me with soft eyes and a genuine smile.

"You know, you ought to write a book about your travels."

"I'm planning on it," I said. "You wouldn't believe the crazy stuff that's been happening."

"You'd be surprised. Do you believe in the extraordinary workings of the Divine Spirit?" she asked.

I wasn't sure how to respond. Was she trying to recruit me for some religious sect? She read my skeptical expression.

"You're not the only one asking questions," she said. "Here, take my card." She slid one across the table. I flipped it over. It read: *Atlas Securities*.

"Maybe I do believe," I said, though I didn't tell her my last name. "This might sound odd, but I think I'm searching for a crystal. While I was driving down here I felt an odd sensation in my lips similar to what I've felt while holding certain gemstones, especially smoky quartz. I'd like the crystal to be a symbol of my time in Colorado. Do you know where I can find a piece of quartz that was mined nearby?"

"As a matter of fact, I do." Grabbing a pad, she drew a crude treasure map to Manitou Springs, a town about an hour's drive north.

Back on the road, at Manitou Springs I parked my car on the main drag and ran through back allies visiting a few obscure gem and mineral shops. Coming up empty, I made my way toward the center of town where I wandered upon the Whispering Winds, a small, well-lit, occult bookstore. There, the salesman assured me that his wife—a "fifth-generation shaman"—could answer any question I had, provided I returned in a half-hour.

"She's on her lunch break," he said. "Shamans gotta eat, too."

While waiting, I visited one last gem shop. It was a run-down, dusty place, ironically situated right where I'd parked my car. In my haste, I had failed to notice it. Within seconds of entering the shop, my eyes landed upon a nondescript chunk of gray quartz mined from a nearby mountain. Careful not to be impulsive, I earnestly inspected all the shelves, doing my best to ignore that particular stone. When I finally picked it up, I received such a tremendous jolt that I nearly fell backward. I paid two dollars for the rock—it had been marked down from four—before returning to Whispering Winds.

Holding the quartz tightly, I browsed through books on psychic phenomena and admired the feathers and rattles adorning the walls. A woman in her mid-50s with long, dark hair approached me from behind. I knew it was the shaman, and her presence immediately produced strong vibrations in my temples and over the crown of my head. Turning to face her, I asked her about the sensation in my lip.

She looked me up, down, and circled around me as if she were reading my soul. When she spoke, her voice was serious.

"The sensation you're feeling is due to a sudden separation."

My mind flashed to Penelope, who was on her way back to Georgia. I was nervous, as it suddenly dawned on me that I was all alone with an enormous journey ahead of me.

"Not to worry, kiddo," she said in a motherly way. "Everything's going be all right. Take this book."

She handed me a small paperback entitled "Practical Telepathy."

"That'll be fifteen dollars," she said, grinning.

I handed over the money, gave her a hug, hopped back in the car, closed the book on Colorado and set my sights on Alaska.

CHAPTER 9
THE FISHBOWL

I WASTED NO TIME backtracking across the stark landscapes of Utah and Nevada before swinging north through California, Oregon and Washington. Finally crossing the border into British Columbia, at the checkpoint I picked up a young, light-traveling hitchhiker from Montana who was on his way to Vancouver. Landing at a lively coffee shop downtown, I told him all about my journey and new exploration of psychic energy sensitivity. I prodded him with questions about his rural upbringing, imagining that perhaps he had learned of such esotericism during contemplative time in the wilderness, whereas fast-paced city life had muted my own abilities.

"I don't know about all that," he said, "but I hope you're writing it all down."

Then, in an instant, he abruptly tilted his head forward and feverishly vibrated his lips together. It produced a buzzing sound that, curiously, activated the sensation in my own lips.

"What was that?" I said. Clearly there was more to him than met the eye.

"What was *what*?" he responded, raising an eyebrow and a half-smile.

We spent the night at a youth hostel where he told me stories of the rugged, northwest provinces. In the morning, as I climbed into my car, he approached me for another ride to his friend's place on the opposite end of town. We drove a few miles through the city before parking behind a small, vintage mobile home on a quiet, dead-end street. Grabbing his backpack, he disappeared inside a basement apartment next door and that was the last I saw of him.

Still searching for some fresh, British Columbia pot to ease the boredom of the arduous passage ahead, I happened upon the neighbor's porch where a number of bleary-eyed contemporaries sat smoking an enormous spliff in broad daylight. The porch itself was a sight to behold, cluttered with ragged couches, empty, ring-stained coffee cups and overflowing ashtrays. The surrounding walls blared bright yellow with intermittent, dark green panels. The billows of cannabis smoke added a certain mystique, and the place oozed with character. In between puffs I met Sammy, a Kiwi raised in Australia who claimed he was dodging two thousand dollars in unpaid parking tickets down under.

"I'm not going back there," he said stoically in his thick Aussie accent. "I'm not going back, period. Traveling is a state of mind, man. You stay in the *now* and you can always go forward."

Barefoot and dressed in tattered, Indian-inspired garb that complemented his flowing, tan dreadlocks, his dark brown eyes shined with the promise of utopia as he spoke of an approaching trip to a Rainbow Gathering in the Kootenay Mountains. Sitting next to Sammy, who couldn't have been a day over twenty, it felt like nothing had ever existed prior to that moment and nothing would ever exist beyond it.

"Would you like to come to the gathering?" he asked earnestly. He seemed prepared to share his entire life with me should I say "yes."

"When are you leaving?" I said.

"I cannot speak for the future," he said. "But soon."

It suddenly occurred to me that he needed a ride, and he was masking the guilty expression of someone evading responsibility at all costs. Sadly, I had to decline, but nevertheless was persuaded to spend a night at the "Fishbowl," the traveler-friendly home of a cyber-junkie and psychedelic prince named Fish, whose moldy outdoor furniture provided ample sleeping space and exotic smells galore. That same evening he housed five other travelers free-of-charge, including Ben, a young Quebecker who was busy crafting didgeridoos out of bamboo he'd harvested from a neighbor's garden. While he whittled, he spoke candidly of his bout with schizophrenia that had previously landed him in the psych ward for two months.

"I saw orbs floating in the streets," he said, slightly embarrassed.

"What's wrong with that?" I said.

"Nothing, really. I felt fine, but I couldn't recognize my own mother."

"Oh."

"At least not until they got me off LSD and onto their meds. Now I feel crappy and the orbs are gone, but my mom and sister are speaking to me again."

Having recovered his "right" mind, he said, he was now receiving government aid and working on "being here now." Ben pointed to his lap where rested a curious purple book by Ram Dass encouraging him to do just that.

"It's no coincidence that you've arrived here," he said. Ben opened the book wide and pressed a single page toward my face. It read in large print, "It's the vibrations *you* give off."

Maybe this is why I'm meeting all these eccentrics, I thought. *My energy is attracting them.*

As if on cue, Linda poked her head outside her trailer to see who was around. A petite woman in her late twenties, she wrapped herself in a thick shawl, stepped onto the porch and quickly struck up a conversation.

"What are you in for?" I joked.

"I'm a Reiki healer," she said.

"Reiki? I've never heard of it."

"Reiki is a healing energy guided by love and compassion. It can't harm you," she said in a gentle, reassuring voice. "The healing can be physical, psychological or spiritual, and there's no telling what you'll feel but, I promise, there's no need to worry."

I explained to her some of the sensations I had been experiencing and told her all about Cuckoo.

"Do you believe in negative energies?" I asked.

"Of course," she said, "and you're right to be cautious. The spiritual world is just as challenging to navigate as the physical one, but you can protect yourself. Visualize a silver light shielding you from head to toe. This will help when you feel that your psychic energy is being meddled with by an outside force."

"How did you get into this stuff?" I asked.

"One day I left home and unexpectedly found myself in a bookstore I'd never visited before. It's difficult to explain, but I felt as if I was being guided there by an unseen hand. I let it sweep me up and was immediately drawn to the very back of the store, where I spotted an unusual book on a bottom shelf. I bought it before I'd even read the cover or knew what I was doing. Upon turning it over, I read: *If you're in possession of this book, you've already made contact with your angels.* Then I started crying."

I nodded, nearly in tears, as I remembered Coretta and the postcard I'd found after our healing session.

"I had an experience just like that," I said.

"The book taught me to call on my angels for help. It also talked about guardian angels that connect two people together in every relationship. Would you like to see for yourself?"

Fully convinced that Linda had only the best intentions, I lied down on a blanket and began to breathe deeply. Her hands moved delicately over my body from chakra to chakra, beginning at the top of my head and proceeding downward toward the soles of my feet. Though her fingertips hovered an inch above my skin, I could feel them pulsing along with each chakra as she guided energy down an invisible channel in the center of my body. By the end of the session, I felt completely relaxed, wide open and alive deep inside. She noted that I had given off a lot of energy and encouraged me to drink plenty of water to help cool down.

Once she'd left, I passed out on one of the grungy couches and awoke early the next morning to find Sammy leaning over me, inches from my face, with a steaming cup of coffee in hand.

"Here you go, brother," he said. "Want to have a smoke?"

I looked at my cell phone, then gazed at the overcast sky. It was 7:30 a.m.

"No thanks, man. I'm gonna hit the road."

"Suit yourself," he said, lighting up another spliff.

Pulling myself together, I noticed how clear and refreshed I felt, devoid of soreness in my neck and back, and moving with the fluidity of water. Knocking on the door, I bid farewell to Fish, still half-asleep but conscious enough to give me his phone number.

"You're welcome back anytime you're in town," he said.

"I don't think I'll be back anytime soon, but thank you so much for your hospitality."

"Hehe, that's what Sammy said the first time he showed up."

Reaching for my car keys, I turned to Sammy. "Goodbye, my friend," I said. "It's been a pleasure chatting with you."

He looked me up and down as if to make sure I was okay to drive, then spoke to me in a deadly serious tone.

"Keep your ear to the ground, man. There's a revolution happening."

CHAPTER 10
ALASKA

IT WAS EARLY EVENING when I arrived in Seward. I had driven ten hours-a-day for five days straight, and was still high on dark roast coffee, having consumed cup after cup for hundreds of miles along the Great Alaskan Highway, or ALCAN. It was Devon's last day of work. I met him deep in the belly of a stinking fish factory, where hordes of Eastern European teenagers on their "dream vacation" to the U.S. had spent the whole summer gutting Sockeyes. By comparison, Devon had had it good, unloading heavy, sealed packages from the conveyor belt. He smelled only slightly of dead salmon but was eager to leave nonetheless. After a quick tour, he tossed his pack in the trunk and we were off through the pounding rain to explore America's last frontier.

From Seward we circumnavigated the Kenai Peninsula to reach Homer, a sleepy town along the coast. We spent a couple days and nights at a cozy youth hostel, admired smoky, Kachemak Bay, picked wild berries, and searched for eagle feathers along the shoreline. From there, we hightailed it to the town of Sterling where we rented a canoe, strapped it to the roof of the car and took it into the Swan Lake system, a vast expanse of unspoiled wilderness. Devon controlled the map and insisted that we portage numerous times in order to reach the largest lake. We arrived at dusk, exhausted. After cooking up a big meal of rice and beans, we paddled out to the middle of the lake at the height of the night, blanketed by darkness and an unrivalled stillness. The tranquility was broken only by the sound of a diving loon sliding across the water on its luminous white belly.

Back in Seward the following evening, Devon and I spent an hour at the library researching *Amanita Muscaria*, or *fly agaric* mushrooms, which we had occasionally spied in the woods all over the peninsula. Despite numerous warnings on campsite message boards urging us to avoid them, we recognized the fleshy, red and white caps from countless fairytales. We picked a few out of curiosity, drying them on the dashboard as we drove.

It didn't take long to discover a trove of folklore attributed to the mushrooms, including claims they were potential *entheogens*, or capable of inducing mystical experiences. Though they required proper preparation and still posed health risks, fly agaric had been used throughout the world for ages in rituals of healing, celebration and war. According to one book, the mushrooms may have even been the legendary *soma* plant and worshiped as a god in parts of ancient India.

After a miserable, three-day trip to Denali, which flicked us off its surrounding hillsides like fleas by way of intolerable hailstorms and oppressive fog, on the eve of our departure back to the mainland Devon and I each ingested a small portion of the mushrooms. We waited by the fire for hours but only felt a little light-headed.

In the morning, we visited some waterfalls nearby. Expecting a mild hike, some nice views, and a final taste of the freshest air on the planet, we'd barely started down the trail when Devon stopped in his tracks.

"Look," he whispered.

The surrounding woods were exploding with fly agaric. It felt like a blessing to stumble upon such a sight, the emerald forest floor bursting with color. Tiptoeing through the trees, we picked the ripe mushrooms.

"Don't over-pick," said Devon with a hint of authority, though he was equally awe-inspired, his hazel eyes shining brightly.

"It's like a dream," I said.

Carefully cleaning the mushrooms and stashing them in an old cookie tin, we got back on the ALCAN and managed our way down through the Yukon over the course of a week. As we drove, we spotted black bears, a bighorn ram, caribou, elk and buffalo, and witnessed an unprecedented display of aurora borealis streaking across the starlit tundra.

Our plan was to visit national parks all the way to South Dakota, but Jasper, in Alberta, was overly crowded with agitated, ice-cream-cone-eating tourists piling in and out of their minivans. Between all the entry fees and taxes, it seemed like we were paying by the minute. By the time we reached Banff, we knew something had to give.

"I've got to see the redwoods," Devon pleaded. "I don't know when we'll get out here again and I've wanted to do this my whole life. We're so close!"

"We're practically in Montana!" I said, "and we're due in New York next week."

I pored over the map in search of a solution. The closest redwoods were a thousand miles away—in the opposite direction—yet our decision was black or white: we head east, or we head west. My entire journey flashed before my eyes.

This whole trip is about freedom, I thought.

Then I imagined Coretta's face smiling at me, egging me on. *It could all be over in an instant.*

"Alright. Let's do it!" I said.

Devon's face lit up.

"That a'boy!" he said, and off we rode.

Ten hours later we were in Vancouver, arriving at 3 a.m. with nowhere to go except Fish's flophouse. We hadn't called ahead, so he wasn't expecting us. We humbly knocked on the door. A minute later, he answered. He was naked, delirious, and heading to bed.

"Hey! You're back," he said, "and you brought a friend." He rubbed his weary eyes. "We're all full up, though."

Looking around, I saw that the cozy porch furniture and every inch of floor space was already occupied.

"You can sleep on the front lawn if you want," he said.

He pointed to a ten-by-ten patch of grass adjacent to the sidewalk. Devon and I wasted no time unrolling our sleeping bags.

At sunrise, we awoke to a stunning view of downtown Vancouver. After a brief to-do with some undercover cops who likened us to suspects in a pre-dawn burglary—one of the pitfalls of sleeping on the street, we reasoned—we enjoyed another glorious day in the Fishbowl, buzzing with electricity in anticipation of a neighborhood-wide festival that Fish was throwing in his backyard later that afternoon. We helped make the salsa with our bare hands and hung around just long enough to eat some before climbing back in the car and heading south through the night.

Driving through a torrential thunderstorm in Washington, we didn't stop for eighteen hours until we reached Humboldt County, California. The last stretch on Route 299 from Redding to the coast was especially precarious, weaving along switchbacks through the lush, Shasta-Trinity wilderness. Espresso and adrenaline were the only things keeping us going. As we drove, I wondered if I had shaved a year, or several, off my life from all the sleep deprivation I'd endured that summer. My body begged for a complete overhaul after what seemed like an eternity at the wheel.

In Arcata, a town moving at a rhythm all its own, we found our way to the plaza where twenty or so homeless people lingered. All of them were roughly our age. We were told they made up a "Rainbow Family" that had emerged from a gathering and had taken up residence in the redwood forest just north of town. As they received hot food from a couple of volunteers, a young man named Mud played guitar and sang a bluesy song about not being able to return home to "reality." I sympathized with him, as waking life was beginning to seem more like a fascinating delusion to me as well.

After dark, Devon and I snuck into a big redwood campground near Trinidad. In the morning, we drove further north to Prairie Creek State Park. The sight of the mammoth trees took our breath away. At Prairie Creek, we hiked five miles among the giants before landing on the coast for a golden sunset over the Pacific blue. The wispy evening tide lulled us to sleep, and we awoke to a slow, steady September drizzle that shrouded the preternatural forest in silver mist. I bounded out of the tent full of energy, wanting to sing, dance and run around. Following breakfast, we walked up the beach a few miles before turning back into the woods, where we came upon a damp, dank, mossy grove. The air was thick with an odd musk.

"Something feels different here," I said to Devon, who was a few paces ahead of me.

"Don't move," he said, spooked.

A colossal, bull elk with prodigious antlers—like broadswords sharp as razors—appeared a few feet to our right, stopping us dead in our tracks as we came around a bend.

"If there's one thing I know for sure," said Devon, "it's that you don't cross a bull elk in mating season."

Carefully backing away, we sat for thirty grueling minutes, listening to a variety of loud grunts and groans. As it turned out, the entire area was inhabited by loads of the enormous creatures seeking privacy for their annual rut.

"It's like a cheap motel," I said.

Devon bit his lip, straining not to laugh.

"*Shhhhh,*" he whispered. "Show some respect!"

Having escaped the redwoods, we barreled north up the Oregon coast, then east through the Columbia River Gorge. We didn't stop to relax much through Washington other than taking a sunset jaunt along some railroad tracks that ran through rolling farmlands. In Walla Walla, we ate greasy cheeseburgers at an old diner filled with Marlboro smoke and locals in overalls and bright green, John Deere hats. The patrons pretended to ignore us and surely got a kick out of watching the haggard strangers drop nickels into the booth-side jukebox. We spent a night camping under evergreens in rural Idaho, followed by a morning in Missoula, Montana, where the whole town was at the college football game atop the hill. After some decent coffee, we'd driven two miles out of town when, without warning, the passenger-side window of my car fell off its hinges with a *thunk* and was lost inside the door.

"There's no way we can drive like this!" I hollered to Devon.

He laughed hysterically, enjoying the sudden gust of wind through his oily, matted hair. Doubling back to town, we persuaded a local mechanic to help us even though it was Saturday afternoon and he was busy listening to the radio.

"I got just the thing for you fellas," he said when he finally acknowledged us. His superlative duct-tape job would last us the rest of the way.

South Dakota showed us the otherworldly Badlands, followed by a hardy breakfast of blueberry pie and a five-cent cup of coffee in a one-stop town called Wall. Pausing for an hour or so to appreciate the big sky in Blue Earth, Minnesota, we spent a night visiting a friend in Northfield and another with my sister in Madison, Wisconsin, where she was in her final year of college. The next afternoon we caught six innings of a Cubs game at Wrigley Field for ten bucks-a-piece. When the game finished early, we drove fifteen hours straight through the black night to New York City before crashing down at my parents' Upper West Side apartment as the day's first light crept through the seventh-story windows. My folks, rudely awakened from the commotion, were noticeably confused by our unheralded return.

"You didn't know we were coming?" I said, grinning widely.

"Whoops!" said my father.

He was happy to see me but, judging by his frazzled expression, wondered who was this scruffy-faced, bleary-eyed vagabond that had suddenly descended upon his doorstep.

CHAPTER 11
THE LOTUS LEAF

FIVE MONTHS AND 20,000 MILES later, I returned to New York with a backpack full of slide film. Devon caught a flight to Florida, and I set to work getting the rolls developed. As I'd traveled I had protected the film like a treasure, storing it on ice in a cooler in the trunk of my car for fear of heat damage beneath the relentless summer sun. I had no plans for the future and felt like my entire life was resting on the strength of my photographs.

On the afternoon the film was ready, I locked myself in my bedroom, wore silk gloves, and delicately flipped through slide after precious slide. There were over a thousand in total, and I meticulously separated out the ones that struck me as valuable, either sentimentally, aesthetically or both. Occasionally, I stopped to reflect on a memory, moment, or a beautiful portrait, many of them moving me to tears. I found it curious that, having spent much of my childhood sorting through baseball cards in search of the rare ones, here I was partaking in a virtually identical ritual.

A few hours later, I emerged with roughly thirty images, about one per roll, that I thought were the best. I felt an incredible sense of relief that not only had the film survived, but I also had something to show for my efforts. Inspired by the "catch," I was eager to get to work on the next phase of the project, assembling the images and stories into a book or some sort of portfolio that I could parlay into a job. I had no clue how long this would take, and my resources were nearly depleted. I knew I couldn't go back to the law firm. I also knew I couldn't live with my parents anymore. I was drunk on freedom, and they were beginning to breathe down my neck.

Determined to not let the city get me down, I stayed true to my goal and spent what was left of my savings on a computer, slide scanner, light box and printer. It was then that my father, who had always wanted to be an artist but had been denied the opportunity by his dad, suggested that I spend the winter house-sitting in the snowy, Berkshire mountains of Western Massachusetts. Two years prior, my folks had bought an old farmhouse to serve as a summer home but hadn't spent more than a few weeks there at a time. Eager to continue my work in solitude, I leaped at the invitation. Moving in around the first of December, I set-up my studio in a spare room and re-immersed myself in my fantasy world.

The house was situated on a dirt road surrounded by dense woods and was twenty miles from the nearest grocery store. I went long stretches without seeing or speaking to anyone. I often stayed up all night transcribing journal entries, reliving the vivid details of one event after another, and recalling the defining experiences that truly expressed the spirit of my adventure.

At the same time, I began to study the work of great photographers whose books my father had collected over the course of his life. Each night I chose a new teacher, from

Stieglitz to Steichen, Evans to Eggleston, Ansel Adams to Edward Weston, Gary Winogrand and Margaret Bourke-White. Scouring over their aesthetics and feeling for the emotional impact of their work, I painstakingly searched for similar elements in my own. It was Henri Cartier-Bresson, who wrote in detail about capturing the "decisive moment," that I felt the greatest kinship with. At times, it felt like he was sitting right beside me offering encouragement.

It was also during those dark, enchanted nights that I started to deepen my yoga practice, regularly moving through the few postures and routines I had picked up in college, on the road and during the handful of classes I'd attended in New York. I knew that I had only begun to scratch the surface and that there was a lot more to it than stretching and breathing. Then, one evening after a particularly tiring hike through thick snow, I stood in the center of the living room and caught a glimpse of whatever it was I had been seeking. My body was agonizingly stiff and sore. Within thirty minutes of concentrated practice, however, all my aches and pains vanished spontaneously into thin air, as if they had been flushed out of my being completely. In the center of my chest I felt a vast expanse of space, a gaping wellspring pulsing with soothing, vibrant life force like warm honey. The phone rang and startled me, as I wasn't quite on the Earth in that moment. It was my father calling to check-in, and I shared the news.

"Good, I'm happy for you," he said, not quite grasping the significance of the experience but genuinely excited for me. As we spoke his voice softened and I was convinced he could feel whatever was moving through me—that there was a special resonance between us that seemed to transcend our physical separation. Then, as we prepared to hang up, there was a long pause.

"There's something I need to tell you," he said.

"Yes, Dad?"

"Don't ever stop *loving,* Son. That's your gift."

The sensation in my chest overwhelmed me, and I wept like a baby. Later that evening I began to pray, both in my mind and via notes in my journal, for a true yoga teacher to enter my life and show me the way.

*   *   *

After about a month as a hermit I knew it was time for a break, so I returned to New York City for the holidays. On Christmas Eve I met up with Devon, who had flown up from Florida to visit. Together, we attended a concert put on by a band called The Slip, whose eclectic music and tight-knit community overlapped with Sound Tribe's. During intermission, we stepped out into the chilly, dimly lit night for some fresh air. My eyes landed upon the beautiful, young woman that had disappeared from my life without a trace the previous summer. It was Annabelle, peering back at me from beneath her dark, hooded sweatshirt. Crouching in a graffiti-laden doorway, her face looked pale and her demeanor was muted. Frozen with fear, I ducked away from the scene to consult with Devon and figure out how to play it.

"You should go talk to her," he said.

"I know, I know," I stammered as wonderful memories flooded my mind and dormant emotions awakened. "But this could be *it*. I don't even know what *it* is, but she might be the 'one.'"

"Why are you freaking out?" he said. "It's just fate— nothing to worry about."

"Let's get a cup of tea," I said, eager to run and hide.

Around the corner, we each drank a cup of chai which helped calm my nerves before returning to the scene outside the club. Annabelle was still tucked inside the doorway. I approached cautiously. Stepping down from the stoop, she kissed my forehead and pressed herself against me.

"I wasn't sure what to do," she whispered in my ear apologetically. "I never made it to California, and I didn't know how to find you."

"I was afraid you'd forgotten about me," I said.

She squeezed me tighter still, determined not to let go this time. The world around us grew quiet as we listened to our heartbeats synchronize. The rest of the scene appeared to fall away.

"Meet me on New Year's Eve?" she said.

I nodded.

After the concert, Devon returned home, and I prepared for my date with Annabelle. We met at a small lounge on Houston Street in the West Village. A handful of old friends accompanied me there, but she and I ducked out early and strolled along the Hudson River for hours. Then, sitting on a rope net in a children's playground, she leaned over and kissed me for the first time. With the arrival of dawn, we watched the sunrise through the cracks between the buildings and walked miles to her favorite Lower East Side diner for banana pancakes. She slept on my lap in a cab heading uptown and we spent the rest of the day curled up in bed.

She seemed larger than life. Lying there for hours, our bodies pressed together, I began to feel immense pressure in my chest, as if my heart was enlarged and going to explode out of my body. I felt completely vulnerable, and when I looked into her eyes, I ceased to see the attractive woman I'd fallen for. Rather, I saw a cavernous, playful, compassionate soul that seemed to engulf me. I saw her as a whole being, void of gender and even time or place. I withdrew in fear.

"Don't worry, baby," she said reassuringly. "It's love."

"It's intense," I said. "It's like we're inside of one another."

"I know," she said. "This is me. It's what I do."

She continued to hold me, stroking my head, and gradually I settled down.

A few days later she returned to school in Boulder, I retreated to the Berkshires, and our relationship continued over the phone, which grew challenging very quickly. Right after she left I got sick, which made me question whether I was on the right path. My heart ached ferociously with loneliness. I decided to call Devon to discuss my dilemma. Our conversation was relatively normal until I felt a sudden jolt of electricity rush through my body. My eyes closed involuntarily, my breath steadied, and Devon changed his tone on a dime.

"Good," he said. "Now you're really listening."

I was stunned. *Can he feel my level of presence over the phone?*

"I have a message for you," he said.

His voice had become slow and cryptic, and every cell in my body stood at attention.

"The Annabelle of the present will bring you your highest highs," he said, "but afterward you'll fail to return there. The Annabelle of the future, however, will bring you your ultimate contentment."

Though his words took me by surprise, I knew exactly what he meant. It was like speaking with a psychic medium. Just as precipitously as the peculiar energy had arrived, it seemed to dissipate, and our conversation returned to a conventional chat. It was almost as if the moment hadn't happened at all. The seed had been planted, however, and it began to eat at me.

Unable to sleep, I called Annabelle and told her that we needed to break it off. I made no mention of Devon's message. The pain we each experienced was excruciating, and I felt awful for blindsiding her.

"What do you mean we're breaking up?" she sobbed. "We're in love. I can feel it!"

"I feel it too. I've never met anyone like you, but I can't stand the pain of not being with you. It's throwing my life out of balance." I struggled to hold back my tears.

"I know it hurts, baby. I want to be with you so badly. You could move out here."

"No. I don't want to move."

"Why not?"

"I don't know. It's just too soon."

"What does your heart say?"

I paused, listening for a message telling me to run to her. It never came.

"My heart says this is goodbye, at least for now."

I bit my lip and heard her weeping on the other end of the line. There was a long, uncomfortable silence, then she hung up abruptly. I sunk to the floor with sadness. I was alone again.

In the days and weeks that followed, I rededicated myself to my work in an effort to block out the pain. Annabelle and I stopped speaking to one another and communication with my parents, who couldn't come to terms with my lifestyle, was increasingly strained. Apart from Devon, I felt like no one understood me. Ironically, as my waking life relationships began to erode, it seemed as if the part of my consciousness that was active during sleep was awakening to its full potential. Eager for companionship, I would often lie in bed and silently invite friendly spirits to visit me in dreams. Occasionally, I'd receive an answer.

One night I began to dream that someone was snuggling up along my right side, pushing me very sensually in my midsection. It was Annabelle. Before I knew what was happening, I felt myself floating upward and out of my body, yet I remained fully aware that I was asleep and even snoring slightly. Suddenly, I saw her clear as day, sitting on a white cloud amidst a dark sea faintly visible beneath us.

"I wish we could share this together," I said to her.

She smiled back at me lovingly.

"We can," she said. "Just *be* in the heart!"

In an instant, my bedroom was illuminated in a flash of shimmering silver light that lingered for a second or two. When it faded, to my amazement, my consciousness was hovering inches beneath the ceiling. I had a bird's eye view of the entire room and looked down at my sleeping body. A loud, high-pitched ringing sound filled the air. Having previously read up on out-of-body experiences, I tried to focus on various objects in an effort to prolong my flight, but I panicked at the thought of my body's immobility and was sucked back in like a vacuum.

After that, my nightly visions continued to evolve until out-of-body experiences and lucid dreams became commonplace. In time, I learned that my vivid dreaming wasn't specific to Western Massachusetts. While attending my sister's graduation from college that May, I felt especially alienated from the rest of my family, all of whom ate meat and drank more heavily than me. Over the winter, in an effort to amp up my spiritual energy, I'd begun experimenting with vegetarianism and had cut back on all substances, especially alcohol. Consequently, while everyone was out celebrating, I turned in early to brood.

Soon, I dreamt that I was at a festival where two unfamiliar, nondescript men confronted me.

"Are you a leader?" asked one of them.

"Yes," I answered bluntly.

They looked at me skeptically.

At this point in the dream I could feel my sister's presence alongside me though I couldn't see her. I woke up briefly but immediately fell back asleep and dreamt that I was standing next to a tall wooden tower. Atop the tower stood the same two men. To their right were two large birds with spectacular golden beaks.

I looked up at the men. They peered back at me indifferently.

"I've lost my parents," I said.

The two men conversed with each other, before one of them turned to me.

"Meet them at the 'Lotus Leaf,'" he said.

Somehow, I knew the "Lotus Leaf" was an actual place on the opposite side of the festival grounds and I could see it in my mind. Inside there was a remarkable wooden bridge, which I also knew was significant though I didn't know why.

"Can't I meet them at 'Fate?'" I asked. "Fate" was another booth on the edge of the grounds much closer to us.

"No, the Lotus Leaf!" they insisted.

At that moment a magnificent, illuminated eagle flew overhead, and to the left of where the two men had stood were two baby eagles with sparse hair on their heads and wings. I never saw the birds and the two men together, as they appeared individually in flash-frames, so it's possible that they were one in the same.

When I awoke to write down all that I'd seen, I knew intuitively that to "Meet them at the Lotus Leaf" meant to meet them in the heart—to meet them with love. I also truly felt that I had visited a special world, a real place existing parallel to our own, and was reminded of a pair of hawks that had flown past me and my parents during a rose-colored, Massachusetts sunset a couple months earlier. It had been a memorable, shared experience—an omen for each of us—and was one of the few in recent memory during a period where we had less and less in common.

Chapter 12
Alberto Montana

DEVON AND I DECIDED to retrace our steps across the country. Sound Tribe was playing all the same spots, and we reasoned it would be smooth sailing, as we were a little older and a little wiser, albeit a little broke. Having packed a small backpack full of clothes, my camera, and several rolls of film, I printed a single copy of the book I had been working on all winter and left the Berkshires for Tennessee.

Back at Bonnaroo for the third year in a row, on Friday morning I set out to find Annabelle, who had left a message on my cell phone a few days earlier. I was excited to hear her voice after months without contact. She said she'd be at the festival with her friends, camping beneath a large, red octopus balloon. Though Bonnaroo had only grown larger and more difficult to navigate, I suspended reason, honed-in on her "signal," and located her tent within half-an-hour. When she saw me, she dropped what she was doing and ran over to embrace me. I knew that she intended to convince me that we should be together. Neither of us knew exactly where we were heading after the festival. Sure enough, she asked if she could accompany me out West. I told her I'd have to think about it.

Later that afternoon, Devon and I snuck into the music area by taping together scrap pieces of neon, plastic bracelets in order to deceive the security guards. Once inside, we wandered in opposite directions, and I found my way to a large, grassy meadow full of new age info booths and artist tents. Outside one such tent I met Alberto Montana, a famous psychedelic artist. Montana, who was revered within the Sound Tribe scene, had displayed several large prints of his work across the white tent walls and was promoting the Psychedelic Art Network, or PAN, which he spearheaded. Much of the work depicted spiritual visions received from entheogens, which the network praised for their unequivocal powers of inspiration.

Captivated by his magnetism and eager to share my own work, I handed him my book. He flipped through it casually, admiring the photos but glossing over the stories.

"You have a good eye," he said. "You should dream big. You're as big as you dream you can be."

"Thank you," I said, flattered.

"You'll have to be an artist for ten years to become a master, though."

I nodded.

"Sometimes I look at all the work I've done," he said, "and I think I must be insane."

He laughed awkwardly before his assistant interrupted us and diverted Montana's attention elsewhere.

As I walked off, I had the unnerving feeling that he was watching me even after I'd returned to the campgrounds, over a mile away. I tried not to dwell on my suspicion, however, and was excited to have met him. Later that evening, compelled by the desire to be around genius should it perhaps rub off on me,

I returned to Montana's booth where I was welcomed and offered a seat beside him.

"The man of the hour has arrived," said Montana.

Montana inched his chair closer to mine and his assistant sat down to the left of him. Within a few moments I began to notice a profound and unexpected shift in consciousness, as if the waking world was transforming into the dream world right before my eyes. Colors, shapes and sounds began to dance all around me. My breath steadied, and I perceived an illuminated, golden triangle in the center of my forehead—something I had never seen before. As I became more meditative, my attention was drawn to one of Montana's paintings hanging inside the tent.

"Good choice," I thought I heard him say. "Yes, you *heard* me just fine," said his telepathic voice in my mind.

The voice was accompanied by the faint yet unmistakable sound of tribal drumming reverberating throughout my body. Despite my confusion, as everything was happening very quickly, I understood that he was leading me on a psychic, shamanic journey, although I had no frame of reference for such an experience. I realized he had invaded my mind. My body shook with a peculiar mix of dread and curiosity. Not only could I hear Montana's silent voice, but I could also hear his assistant's. A short, devious-looking young man with a cackling laugh, he reminded me of a dark, mythical creature, like a goblin. In overhearing their own telepathic conversation, it occurred to me that Montana was teaching his disciple to *see*—to read the emanations of the "energy body"—and I was that evening's lesson.

Gripped with both fear and excitement, I lied down on the ground and my body became nearly immobilized. I tried in vain to assimilate the overpowering sensations of foreign energy rushing through me. I felt Montana's foot press gently against my left shoulder as I sunk deeper into the grass. Helpless, I watched the two of them *see* my every thought, repressed memory, trauma, and hidden desire. It was as if they were opening up the hidden closets of my soul, one by one. My body shook furiously as I tried to fight them off in my mind.

"Just let go, son," I heard Montana say. "This is my *work*. It will make you stronger."

Taking a deep breath and attempting to relax, an image of Annabelle flashed through my mind's eye.

"Don't be serious!" scoffed Montana's silent voice. "She'll only slow you down."

Before long, I felt as if they had accessed my entire being. There was nowhere left to hide. I was petrified. Adding insult to injury, I sensed that Montana was disappointed in me.

"He can't see that Alberto is *painting*," said his assistant to some onlookers who had gathered around us. I could hear them all joking about my being "blind." Through all of this, however, I continued to focus my mind on the glowing, golden triangle still pulsing in the center of my forehead. I was determined to prove myself worthy.

After what seemed like hours of punishing concentration, I felt a strange rumbling throughout my body. Suddenly, all the energy I'd compressed in my third eye shot downward into the center of my chest. I heard what sounded like a camera flash and, simultaneously, witnessed an explosion of energy out of my heart. In an instant, my entire awareness was consumed by infinite shards of shimmering, white light, and an inimitable feeling of release.

"You're beautiful!" said Montana.

It was, in fact, the most beautiful thing I had ever seen. It was *me*!

Unfortunately, the brilliant light only lasted a few moments. Once it had dissolved, Montana seemed to grow tired of me, and I could feel him urging me to leave. Terrified and embarrassed yet astonished by the ineffable vision and still tingling with ecstasy, I finally garnered the courage to break free. As I gathered my belongings and stumbled off into the darkness, I once again heard Montana's silent voice in my mind.

"Quesadillas," he laughed. "Quesadillas."

Somehow, I knew he was alluding to my makeshift, plastic bracelet that would not fool the guards the following day.

The next afternoon, the security intensified and I was forced to sit with Devon under a pop-up tent in the parking lot during a pounding thunderstorm. As the rain poured down hour after hour, I stared aimlessly at his homemade vending sign that read *Quesadillas*. To Devon's credit, he tried as best he could to cheer me up—it was a music festival, after all—but it was no use. I was devastated.

Once the rain let up, I ran into Tristan, who I hadn't seen since he'd dropped us off in Boulder the previous summer. He sensed my unease and sidestepped the usual chit-chat, handing me a deck of tarot cards instead. Carefully shuffling the deck, on my first attempt I pulled a card that read *Schizophrenia*. It displayed the image of a young man dangling in thin air and grasping to cliffs on either side, torn between two worlds. Moments later, the sky turned dark and crackled, and it started pouring rain again.

By Sunday morning I perked up a bit after procuring a used bracelet from a girl who'd left early, enabling me to slip past security. Once inside the stage area I made a b-line for Montana's booth. I was motivated by a manic fervor to find out what had happened to me. However, as I approached his tent, a sudden thunderstorm forced him and his team to break down their set up. Having already succumbed to the elements, I sat and watched as Montana and his crew rushed nervously to secure their possessions and escape the rain. There was a part of me that delighted in watching them suffer.

When the storm passed I reunited with Annabelle, who I hadn't seen since the first morning. She still hadn't fixed her plans and pleaded for us to travel cross-country together. I told her I couldn't, a decision based in large part on Montana's message about her, though I had begun to doubt myself and didn't know how I truly felt. Standing beside a wooden fence at the edge of a field, she began to sob and collapsed onto the grass, her elegant frame curled up in a ball. I watched her tears drip down into the soaked earth.

108

CHAPTER 13
THE COUNTRY FAIR

A LOOSELY-AFFILIATED GROUP of fifteen or twenty
nomads, we followed Sound Tribe across the country.
Occasionally, we would run into each other at gas stations,
restaurants, campgrounds and swimming holes, as if divine
providence had brought us together. On the weekends, we'd
reconvene at festivals in Kansas, Colorado, or California, and
greet each other like family. Unphased by great distances and
uninterested in our pasts, we believed that we were an integral
part of something revolutionary, albeit undefinable.

The band began to notice us and would invite us backstage
to hang out. Those moments seemed outside of time. Having
already met Hunter at Bonnaroo, I seized the opportunity to
speak with the remaining band members. David Murphy—or,
Murph, who played bass—nodded in approval as he flipped
through my book attentively.

"You guys are such an inspiration," I said, hoping to break
the ice.

"Don't worry about what *we're* doing," he said, motioning
toward my camera. "Focus on what *you're* doing!"

The trouble was, I didn't know what I was doing, nor what
forces I was meddling with. Alberto Montana had upended my
world, and I couldn't shake him from my memory. He had
stripped me of my innocence, or perhaps my ignorance, and I

no longer felt safe. What had started as a meaningful journey increasingly felt like aimless wandering.

Devon and I parted ways in mid-July. Sound Tribe was taking a break, and he was off to Hawai'i to meet up with Aja, the woman with the half-butterfly tattoo, who he had kept in touch with all year. Right after he left, I ran into Annabelle in San Francisco. Not wanting to be alone, I tried to persuade her to come with me to the Oregon Country Fair. This time, she turned me down as she was on her own adventure in California and had grown wary of my mercurial heart.

It wasn't difficult to hitch a ride to Eugene. After a few lazy days in town, I arrived at the Fair and was immersed in the quirky scene, which resembled an elfin renaissance festival. Lending to the Country Fair's mystique was their policy that come sundown, everyone without a special permit was required to vacate the grounds. For months, I had heard rumors that a lucky few in possession of a coveted, silver badge—namely, venders, artisans and Fair insiders—were invited to stay through the night, at which point the whole place transformed into a magical wonderland. Legend had it that it might be possible to hide out during the "sweep," a literal cleansing of the grounds by a staff brigade linked arm-in-arm, only to re-emerge after dark for the festivities.

I spent much of my time at the Fair ambling about, sifting through the massive crowds, shooting photographs and attempting to find a badge. As the sun began to set, I had nearly given up when, out of nowhere, a voice called out to me from behind a tapestry alongside the road.

110

"Quick, in here!"

"Tristan!" I shouted.

"*Shhhhh!* Come on!" he whispered.

Looking to make sure the coast was clear, I dashed beneath the tapestries and was pulled down into a small tent. There were at least four other sweaty bodies smooshed against mine. Tristan motioned for us to remain absolutely still, a daunting task as the mosquitoes had begun to make their rounds as well. We heard the procession pass and a short while after that, there was some chatter out on the road. Tristan gleamed with excitement.

"You made it," he said, giving me a nudge. "Go ahead."

Crawling out of the tent, my body stiff and sore from the contortionist act that had been necessary to stay hidden, I inspected the scene. The sky had turned a dusty purple and the massive crowds had dispersed. People dressed like elves, angels, faeries and wizards strolled casually along the paths. The sugary smell of fried dough filled the air and hot elixirs bubbled in large kettles. The mossy, old growth forest draped down all around us, and the occasional hoot of a great horned owl served as a reminder that we were merely guests there. This became my impression of Oregon. I instantly had the feeling I was going to live there.

With the pressure off, I took it easy that evening, sitting beside a campfire for hours listening to a pair of identical twins sing and play guitar. Around 4 a.m., I went to round up some food and met a large man with a flowing white mane and an equally impressive, silvery beard. Seeing my camera, he introduced himself as a fellow photographer and conversed with me while I ate. As I finished my plate, he unexpectedly shifted from his position to face me squarely and moved within inches of my nose, just as Rob Newton had done when he'd taught me about the "Now."

"The day of reckoning is upon us!" he boomed, "and you will be judged by how you make others feel in your presence!"

Though I didn't prescribe to conventional descriptions of the Almighty, given his grandiose appearance, it was like God had come down from heaven to deliver the message, which was probably the look he was going for. Stranger still, upon stepping away from me, he seemed to shrink back to a normal size before proceeding with our conversation as if nothing out of the ordinary had happened.

Bewildered, I wandered off as first light burst through the trees. Suddenly, I heard my name called again. It was Tristan. We caught up over a hot cup of tea.

"So, what do you think?" he said.

"I think I'm going to move out here."

"Gets 'em every time," he laughed. "You're better off heading to Portland, though. There's more happening up there than in Eugene. I'm thinking about landing there too."

Heeding his advice, after the Fair I spent three days in the Rose City. Despite not doing much other than catching up on sleep, I rode a bicycle around the neighborhood, met a few people, and convinced myself to move there come the Fall. Prior to leaving, I made arrangements with some new friends to crash on their couch upon my return, probably around

November. From there I flew back to New York via a stopover in Florida, where I visited my aging grandmother. She took the time to read my psychedelic stories and must have thought I was a total alien but, surprisingly, she encouraged me to keep going.

In Manhattan, my parents had sold their home and were renting a tiny apartment in midtown to get one last taste of city life before retiring to the country for good. As I had nowhere else to go, I stayed in the spare room of their flat with a window overlooking Times Square. I felt horrible there, once again like a prisoner in a small box in the sky.

It began to dawn on me that after another summer of liberal psychedelic use and encounters with a variety of confounding characters, I had opened my mind to such an extent that I'd become highly empathic—a magnet for other people's energy. Even in New York, I attracted all sorts of wayfaring folk, both good and seemingly malevolent. I picked up on their thoughts, experienced their pleasure and pain in my own body, and was often influenced by their emotional state. Sometimes I even heard what sounded like actual radio shows in my head, conspicuously in the moments just prior to falling asleep. Walking the streets, I felt defenseless, weak, delusional, paranoid, and afraid. Subsequently, I spent most of my time in my room, writing, drinking espresso, smoking pot, reading Beat literature, processing photos, and meditating.

My imagination had been stretched to its limits. My family didn't understand me anymore, and I had lost touch with all my old friends except for one, Leo, my best friend from childhood.

He thought I'd gone mad. There were few people I felt comfortable around and, as in the past, Sound Tribe's Lowdown internet forum was my only real outlet. My patience with New York had also worn thin. I could feel the filth and stress of the city in my veins.

Although I'd made up my mind to move out West, in August I submitted a portfolio to the International Center of Photography in Manhattan and was invited to exhibit some of my work there. It was a major boost for my confidence and a sign to my folks that I was working toward something. To prepare for the show, I again retreated to Massachusetts, alone in the woods for several weeks printing, framing, fasting a day or two at a time, and playing around with dream incubation—specifically, welcoming in spirits as I had done previously.

One stormy night in the mountains, I had a terrifying dream of bombs raining down from the sky and exploding over the streets of New York. I could feel the ground shaking and the earth crackling with each blast. Suddenly I shot up in bed, wide awake. Deafening rain was pouring down outside, accompanied by teeth-chattering thunderclaps and streaks of lightning. I sat frozen and shivering for several minutes as the storm grew nearer and nearer. It seemed to be heading straight for the house, and I was concerned that the large maple trees in the front yard might get struck and catch fire or crash through the roof.

There was a moment of pristine stillness, then a blinding flash of light. My hair stood on end as a current of electricity shot up my spine. *BOOM*! A deafening blast of sound dominated the forest. Time stopped. There was a loud, popping noise in the house and I gripped my pillow tightly, praying that everything was okay. Oddly, after the strike the brunt of the storm swiftly departed, and the woods settled down. I pulled myself together and went downstairs to investigate. The oven and stovetop were smoking, presumably from the power surge, but thankfully there were no major disasters to speak of.

Climbing back into bed, my nerves gradually calmed, and I began to drift back to sleep. Looking out the window as my vision grew hazy, I spotted a translucent, blue owl with bright, golden eyes peering back at me from beneath the awning. In my stupor I thought, *Oh, there's an owl seeking shelter from the rain. It's soaking wet, of course, perfectly natural...*

Only in the morning when I remembered the entire incident did I determine that the owl must have been a visitor on the astral plane—as owls typically aren't of the see-through variety. The lightning strike, which was very real, may have been its calling card. In that moment, it felt as if the boundary separating waking and dreaming had completely dissolved, once and for all.

Back in the city, the photo exhibition was well received and after it ended in late September, I spent a final weekend with my parents in Massachusetts to say goodbye. At dusk on my last night, I walked with my father around the edge of the lawn beside the forest. It had been years since we had walked together. I felt like I was transported to a timeless realm. I was his son again, secure in my place just under foot, and I saw the land through new eyes, through his eyes. The woods, grass and sky had specific hues—lavender, burgundy, sage and pine—as if he had painted every last detail with his mind. Even the rocks seemed to speak to me. I became acutely aware of the four directions. I felt as if I occupied one of them all to myself and, inexplicably, felt the presence of my siblings occupying the other three.

"The woods," he said, as if picking up on my thoughts, "the woods are for you."

As he described the intricacies of the trees and spoke of his vision for our home, I realized that I had entered into his dream of Heaven. I was part of his imaginative vision. Tears streamed down my face. He began to cry as well.

"Come here," he said, embracing me.

"Oh, Dad!"

"It's okay, Son. You're letting your heart speak."

CHAPTER 14
THE PAN CALENDAR

ON THE FIRST OF OCTOBER 2004, I packed my car, my sights set on Portland, Oregon, and a fresh start. I didn't have to be there by any specific date, so I decided to take my time traveling across the country and hashed out the most scenic route possible. As there were few campsites between New York and Colorado, I plowed through the Midwest in less than a day, stopping to sleep for a few hours in the driver's seat while a downpour leveled southern Illinois. Phoning ahead to Lawrence, Kansas, I spent a night with a friend I had met at a festival the previous summer, before trudging onto Boulder where Annabelle was waiting for me.

Despite all we had endured, she invited me to stay with her, and we spent several days together. It was obvious to both of us that our love was still present, though we kept our hands to ourselves with the exception of one evening when, after smoking a bit of pot, I was overcome with paranoia. That night she held me close.

"I don't know what's wrong with me," I said, shivering.

"*Shhhhhh,*" she whispered. "Imagine growing roots down into the center of the Earth. It will help you stay grounded."

I rode on. From Boulder, I followed Interstate 70 west through the dazzling, red rock canyonlands of Utah. By chance, I noticed a miniscule, red dot and the words "Hot Springs" on

117

the map where I-70 intersected with I-15. Though I had no idea where I was, I ventured off the main roads in an effort to track them down. Just before dark, I sniffed out the hidden treasure, a small operation called Mystic Hot Springs situated atop a dreary village. When I pulled in I met the owner, Mike, who invited me into the lodge for a cup of tea.

"It's five bucks to soak and another five to camp," he said.

"You can't even buy a slice of pizza for five bucks in New York," I said, handing over the cash.

"We're a long way from New York," he said. "The tubs are open 'round the clock, and you can soak as much as you'd like, anytime you want."

Walking around the lodge, I was amazed to find that every spare inch of wall space was dedicated to music. There were display cases full of blown glass and Grateful Dead memorabilia, including graphic art Mike had created, and the hallways overflowed with signed posters of contemporary acts that had passed through to enjoy the tubs. Apparently, the secret was out amongst the tour buses. I recognized several of the names and faces on the posters and even knew some of the musicians personally. Sound Tribe had visited there too, and it dawned on me that maybe it was no accident I'd discovered the place for myself.

I stripped down and slid into the bubbling hot water, which took my breath away. The springs had been channeled into claw foot bathtubs that were wedged into the side of the cascading rock wall. Each tub looked out over the snow-capped peaks surrounding the dimly lit valley below. As my tension dissipated, crystalline snowflakes began to fall like sparks against the night sky, tingling as they struck my exposed skin. The silence was incomparable.

From the hot springs, I drove south to Zion National Park and pitched my tent in a campground beneath some Japanese maples with bright red leaves. The weather was sunny, and the autumn air was crisp. I spent an entire week exploring the park's abundant waterfalls, hidden creeks and spectacular vistas. From Utah I blazed across Nevada, circumnavigating Las Vegas, which seemed out of place in an otherwise stark, surreal landscape, and continued onto Death Valley, just over the border in southern California. Locating a fine campsite way out in the desert flats, I spent most of my days there seeking shade, visiting landmarks and avoiding tourists. By night, however, I ventured into the desolate, white sand dunes to hike by the light of the full moon.

The dunes themselves were unique in that they only occupied about ten square miles, and with the moon so bright I allowed myself to get lost and let the rolling hills of sand, forever shifting shape, swallow me up. Climbing to the highest peak I could find, I meditated for hours on the sprawling, serpentine forms of the dune crests that seemed an extension of my body. I had read that the sand was essentially finely-ground, quartz crystal, and the locals believed it was full of healing properties. I took a nap there, burying my smoky quartz beneath my head where I'd built up a pillow. Waking several hours later at the height of the blue night, I dug up the crystal. It was warm to the touch. Upon grasping it in my palms, it gave off a brilliant orange spark, sending a tremendous jolt of electricity through my body.

That'll make a good story, I thought, *though few will believe it.*

Arriving in San Francisco on Halloween, exactly two years after Coretta's accident, I linked up with Devon and several other friends from the Lowdown for a series of Sound Tribe shows at the historic Fillmore Theater. After the shows, I spent an extra week in town as there was another party, this one put on by the PAN, scheduled for the following weekend. Only a handful of Sound Tribe's core following hung around for the gathering, which doubled as an exhibition and attracted a select group of young, San Francisco artists and iconoclasts. Upon entering the space, I approached an information table and was handed a flyer that read *PAN Calendar Reform*.

"Do you know about 2012?" asked the wide-eyed, young woman behind the table.

"Nope," I said, though I had heard rumors that the PAN openly embraced the idea that the apocalypse was coming, which spooked me.

"The PAN calendar is a thirteen-month, lunar calendar," she said, "as opposed to the twelve-month, Gregorian calendar we've been told is the most accurate way of measuring time. According to the PAN calendar, in 2012 there will be a spontaneous shift in our collective consciousness as the date marks the end of a *baktun*—a five thousand-year, cyclical period for the ancient Mayans."

"So what's going to happen?" I asked, skeptically.

"No one knows for certain but, by aligning our energies, we'll avoid harm and transcend to another dimension where time is art."

"Fascinating," I said, though I didn't buy it.

Sticking the flyer in my pocket, I ventured further into the room, where Alberto Montana was teaching a drawing class to about fifty participants. The artists that arrived for the class had a particular air about them. Dressed a bit like space-aged pirates in earth-toned, homemade leather outfits, many were adorned with feathers, wore lavish, gemstone amulets wrapped in silver wire and donned suave, full-brim fedoras tipped to the side. Among the crowd were a handful of talented painters that had already received broad recognition for their work. It seemed as if they controlled a hidden volume or intensity among the crowd, both on account of and fueling their magnetism.

At the helm was Montana, a father figure for this younger generation. Already in his late-sixties, he moved slowly and spoke softly yet captivated the audience with his tales of the angelic realms and alien visions that had inspired his work. He conversed openly and eloquently about his long-term fascination with LSD, DMT, MDMA, psilocybin, and ayahuasca, which had us all on the edges of our seats. The idea of "exploring Spirit," as he put it—expanding consciousness and diving deeper into the great mystery—was the zeitgeist and he was on the pulse. When he had finished speaking, I seized a lone opportunity to approach him about our experience together at Bonnaroo.

"Excuse me, Alberto," I said nervously. "Do you remember me from this past summer?"

He glanced at me quickly before looking away.

"Oh sure, Boom Festival, right?" He was referring to a popular, weeklong electronic music festival in Portugal.

"No. Bonnaroo," I said.

I was disappointed that he couldn't place me, and wondered if there were others that had been through what I had.

"Right, right, Bonnaroo," he said.

And then I froze.

"I just wanted to thank you for what you showed me there," I said, tongue-tied.

There was so much I wanted to say to him. Our encounter at Bonnaroo, where he had opened up my mind from the inside-out, had stripped me of my innocence. Ever since, I had felt fear in my heart and was desperate for resolution, yet I lacked the courage to confront him. Sensing my frustration, he withdrew his attention and distanced himself from me.

"I'm glad I could help," he said, before moving on.

A week later, I landed in Southeast Portland and arranged a small nook for myself in the living room of a large house shared by five other people and the owner's young daughter, a redheaded pixie child. Each morning I headed straight for the Red & Black Café, a hipster coffee shop on the corner with good music, tasty espresso and two computers offering free Internet. I spent countless hours watching raindrops trickle down the glass façade while scanning Craigslist for a job and a place to live, managing to secure both after two anxious weeks.

While at the café I flipped through the local tabloid and came across an ad for a PAN-inspired event called the "Infinity Gathering" in Seattle on the weekend prior to Thanksgiving. Neither my job nor my apartment would be available until December 1st, so I booked a flight home for the holiday but decided to drive up to Washington beforehand to check out the scene. When I entered the venue I quickly found that I was underdressed in a hooded sweatshirt and my favorite patchwork pants. Practically everyone was done up in some sort of costume, including an array of silver-haired, glittery-eyed faeries and leather-clad, feather-donning, crystal-wrapping folk.

As I surveyed the space, I realized that the same artists responsible for the previous month's party in San Francisco were behind this event as well. The scene felt darker than Sound Tribe's, more chemically-induced, perhaps. While there were some crossovers, such as myself, I sensed that this tribe, which is what they called themselves, was taking the whole thing a step further with their exploration of psychedelics, consciousness and art. It occurred to me that I was now "traveling" with them and discovering a new branch of the family tree I had begun to climb when I'd first left home. I knew almost immediately that this mysterious limb was shrouded in shadows. Yet, here I was in the thick of it, driven by the same, burning desire to dive deeper down the rabbit hole.

CHAPTER 15
PORTLAND

FOLLOWING A BRIEF TRIP to New York for Thanksgiving, I returned to Portland and settled into a cozy, studio apartment off Northeast Alberta Street—the arts district. During my first night there, I slept directly on the soft, cream-colored carpet and dreamt that I was murdered on a neighboring street.

The next morning, I started my new job as an energy drink salesman. I thought the line of work was particularly ironic seeing as I was so interested in spiritual energy yet was hired to sling powdered electrolytes at the grocery store. The nice part about the job was that I only worked weekends, which gave me ample time to focus on photography and explore the city. Even though I had moved across town, I kept in touch with my friends in the Southeast district who'd hosted me the previous month. One of them invited me to attend a yoga class at Reed College, where she was a student.

"You'll love this guy," she said, referring to the yoga teacher. "He's pretty out there but he really knows his stuff."

"But I'm not enrolled at Reed," I said. "I'll basically be crashing your gym class."

"Don't worry, he won't mind. He might not even notice you."

I'll never forget the day I hopped the gymnasium turnstile and unrolled a purple yoga mat in the back of the warm, dimly lit studio. I admired the polished, bamboo floors, bare auburn walls on three sides, and a fourth wall made entirely of glass that looked out over the woods. I had smoked a little bit of pot prior to my arrival and was feeling pretty mellow in anticipation of what I'd come to expect from a yoga class— some sun salutations, maybe a few balancing postures, a shoulder-stand, and a nice, long relaxation. At first, the other twenty or so students in the class paid me little mind. However, they arranged their own mats into a large circle around the room, as opposed to the single file rows I was accustomed to. I grew a little restless as I was now in full view of not only the students but also the teacher.

Someone is bound to notice the puffy-eyed imposter, I thought.

When the instructor, Stephen, arrived he waved "hello" and positioned himself in the circle alongside us. He was tall, thin and sinewy with a long, black ponytail, a sage-like beard and silver, wire-rimmed glasses. As he was in excellent shape, I couldn't tell if he was in his mid-thirties or his mid-fifties.

"Focus your mind," he said, as he folded his legs beneath him and sat elegantly, his spine long and straight. "We only have an hour-and-a-half to try to achieve something that takes *lifetimes*."

Exhaling forcefully, he began to lead the class through a series of strenuous breathing exercises and loud, Sanskrit mantras. As the official course had begun several months

125

earlier, everyone knew the drill except me. Within a few minutes my head was spinning, and I was on the verge of freaking out, convinced the others could hear my thoughts and were upset by my intrusion. I had been an athlete all my life but had never been challenged physically, mentally and emotionally quite like this. Whatever horse I'd rode in on was stealthily swept out from beneath me, but the reward was the most sensational and humbling relaxation I had ever experienced. Afterward, I snuck out quietly, nodding to the instructor in appreciation and awe. By the time I got to my car, my eyes were wide like saucers and every cell in my body tingled with awareness. I knew my prayers had been answered. The master had finally appeared.

From that day forth, I attended Stephen's classes each Monday and Wednesday afternoon without fail, and practiced the same routine at home on Friday evenings. By February, I was still unsure whether he had realized I wasn't enrolled at the college, so I finally gathered up the courage to speak with him one day after class once I'd finished putting away the mats.

"I want to thank you for letting me join the class," I said, bashfully. "It's different from anything I've ever done before. I just moved out here from New York and have been looking for a teacher for years."

My palms were sweating.

"I'm not sure if you know but"—I gulped, lowering my eyes—"I don't go to school here. Do you mind if I keep coming?"

In that moment he seemed like he was eight feet tall.

"No worries, bro," he said straight-faced, yet knowingly defusing my tension. "Your doing yoga makes my world better."

I peeked up at him, gazing into his razor-sharp eyes for the first time. They were steel gray—wise and deadly serious, yet compassionate, with a touch of mischief.

"You're getting better, too," he added. "Your balance stunk when you first showed up. Your practice is like your jump shot, you know? You can play all the games you want but it's going out there on your own, day after day, and shooting a thousand times that makes the difference."

At the end of each class he would have us all lie down with our heads facing the center of the room and would walk around speaking very softly, asking us to relax our bodies and breathe rhythmically. Vibrations unlike any I had ever felt would trickle down through the crown of my head, dance along my spine and sparkle in the soles of my feet. He was filling us up with magic stuff.

"This is *tantra*," he said, "the yogic art of energy awareness and deep embodiment. It's not all about sex, it's about freedom."

Occasionally, Stephen would casually drop the name of one great yogi or another that he had studied with, such as B.K.S. Iyengar, Pattabhi Jois, and Yogi Bhajan, all of which meant nothing to me at the time. In particular, he often spoke of a revered guru—a spiritual master and genius—that ran a school on some tiny island in Southeast Asia.

"The guru and I play chess," he'd say with a hint of pride.

When I questioned him about the school, he said, "That's the best place for you to go if you *really* want to learn yoga. It's no joke—they don't mess around over there—though I'm not sure how much the guru even teaches anymore."

No matter how many times I brought it up, Stephen never revealed much more than that. The guru remained a mystery to me, and the idea of traveling to Asia was as foreign as, well, Asia. Besides, with Stephen's help I had begun a new kind of adventure, a journey inward, and was thoroughly preoccupied with exploring the sensations, intuitions, synchronicities and visions that were arriving with greater frequency from one day to the next.

Among other practices, Stephen introduced us to a technique called *yoga nidra*—or, "dynamic sleep"—that involved systematically releasing tension and broadcasting healing energy piece by piece throughout and even beyond the body. No other practice impacted me the way yoga nidra did. I usually experimented with it at home on Friday nights, often spending one or two hours lying on the floor, inviting energy into my body, visualizing different colored lights, and waiting for something remarkable to happen. More often than not, I would start to shake violently, abruptly overheat or feel ferocious, shooting pains as energy rose into my skull. Sometimes I feared that I might have a stroke. I voiced my concern to Stephen.

"It's like you're running 220 through a 110," he said.

In other words, my body couldn't handle the *prana*—the life force.

"Do more *asanas*"—yoga postures—"before you lie down to help open up," he said. "And, you've got to change your diet. Eat more organic food."

I followed his advice. By the fifth or sixth month of our time together, I ate my last hamburger, which was a big deal as I had basically lived on fast food from childhood straight through college. It wasn't so much that I'd realized I felt better on a vegetarian diet, which I did, as I simply couldn't stomach red meat and greasy food any more. Yoga was cleaning me out. It was also opening me up to a hidden world.

On rare occasions, Stephen would visit me in dreams. He once appeared as an old hermit with a long, white beard and sat in the lotus posture as he spoke to me with an Indian accent.

"It's wonderful to be with you again," he said. "Too bad it will be so quick this time."

I woke up absolutely certain that he had been my teacher in a previous life and that we'd found each other once again.

On another night he showed up at the end of a much longer sequence of dreams and deposited a drop of bright green liquid on my tongue. Suspecting it was some sort of drug, I asked him about it the following day.

"Wheat grass, bro," he said. I've been meaning to tell you, you should get down on that."

While Stephen was certainly guiding me toward an expanded conception of reality—one that would perhaps help me reunite the two disparate worlds depicted on the ominous "Schizophrenia" tarot card I had drawn at Bonnaroo—he was far from the only teacher I had during that time. The others, however, preferred to use the dreamscape as their classroom. Hardly a night passed when I wasn't dreaming vividly, and a consistent cast of characters would appear time and time again like clockwork. I know, because I recorded every single dream I could remember. Despite spending less time on the Lowdown since I'd left New York, during my time in Portland I grew even closer to Devon, entirely through our dream communication. He would almost always appear on Friday nights to show me something extraordinary, and I logged nearly one hundred separate dreams in which he had a starring role.

One of the first came during my move out West. While camping at Zion National Park, I had dreamt that I was at his home watching him "spin" his chakras by rotating his hands in a clockwise motion a few inches above his chest and belly, similar to Reiki. Several weeks later when I'd settled in Portland, I dreamt that we were driving together along a secret stretch of highway when he instructed me to open the glove box.

"Hand me my 'hot gloves,'" he said.

I had no clue what he was referring to until the next evening when, wide awake and lacking anything better to do, I practiced yoga nidra while holding my smoky quartz crystal against the center of my chest. After a couple minutes I could feel energy swelling in my heart and my palms started burning. I could hear him chuckling in my mind's eye and saying, "Now you get it."

My favorite dream from those first few months in Oregon came one frigid, winter evening—a Friday, naturally—when I met him and several other friends from the Lowdown at Whistler mountain in British Columbia. In the dream, they were encouraging me to dig through the snow. With a little effort, I discovered a sparkling crystal that conjured "*oohs*" and "*ahhs*" amongst them. Upon finding the gem I woke up, but when I fell back asleep moments later I was still with the group, this time in Florida where we were digging through the sand. When I uncovered the same gemstone once again my companions rejoiced, laughing and hugging one another in celebration. As we passed the crystal around they told me, "Touch it and you're healed!"

Interestingly, it was a fairly mundane dream in which Devon showed up wearing a mohawk wig—presumably just to get a laugh—that convinced me I wasn't inventing all this on my own. It was a co-creation, and even this absurd, subtle gesture was an effort to teach me *how* to dream. When I called him to ask whether he'd had the same or similar dreams, he usually responded that he didn't remember them, most likely as a consequence of habitual pot smoking. I wondered, however, if the pot was somehow helping him navigate through the dream world, albeit unwittingly.

When Devon wasn't around to dream with me, there was no shortage of other dreamers, some of them with incredible powers. I frequently dreamt of playing music with Rob Newton. I often felt the sounds resonating inside me, saw silver sparks shooting out from his fingertips, and could even play instruments I'd never touched in waking life with stunning virtuosity. I dreamt of having candid conversations with professional athletes, celebrities, politicians, and even the President. Once I witnessed a Sanskrit symbol emerge from my solar plexus in a spray of bright colors. On another night, I came face-to-face with a hooded cobra, only to discover I was seeing myself as the double helix of DNA. I would often write down dreams only to wake up moments later and realize that the act of writing had also been a dream. Occasionally, I would receive entire prayers and mantras from both strange and familiar visitors.

One Friday night I dreamt that Devon appeared in the form of a duck and urged me to listen very closely.

"Fill me with the healing energy of the Universe, so that I can grow strong and be a bright light onto others," he said.

When I silently repeated the prayer, both while dreaming and later while awake, I felt a special energy that seemed to flow into me from beyond. I dreamt of hummingbirds zooming past my face and hawks flying overhead only to see the same *exact* scenes unfold in waking life the following day. I dreamt a lot about Annabelle, who remained deeply embedded in my heart, and would "look-in" on her at the different locales she visited around the country. Every-so-often, I'd dream of Coretta, meeting her in surreal landscapes and conversing with her effortlessly, as if she had fully recovered from her accident.

On many evenings I would travel to astonishing natural places and meet complete strangers who would offer me gifts, such as amulets, crystals, medicine, and even plants that seemed to glow with a special luster. Sometimes these dream travelers would reveal magical visions with unearthly lights or secret yoga practices I was to try upon waking up. One night I "woke up" in a dream in my own bed and became aware that I wasn't alone. At the edge of my bed sat a young man who shot rainbow lights out of his eyes, heart and hands.

"This will be the experience you'll use to measure all others for the rest of your life!" he said, brazenly.

Suddenly, he transformed himself into the wind and started to shift objects around the room before passing through my body several times, which caused an eruption of pleasurable, albeit obtrusive sensations from head to toe.

Not every dream was enjoyable, however. On odd nights I was visited by aliens, some of them arriving via UFO and others emerging from the ground. Several times I found myself in what appeared to be a "mushroom world," complete with an array of foreign species and outlandish physical laws. I often found these other dimensions disorienting and downright freaky, and in some instances couldn't breathe and felt as if I was being abducted. On more than one occasion it seemed that a creature from these other worlds would tag along with me back to my familiar dream world. I recalled one instance where a small, glowing green entity, not all that different from a magic troll doll, latched onto my arm. As the dream shifted back into my room, the creature multiplied. Before long, the whole room was full of little green trolls, all of them bouncing around and making mischief. While I was fairly certain I had projected the iconic form of the wild-haired doll onto them, I was convinced that there was some sort of autonomous, parasitic creature embodying them.

Concurrent to my ineffable experiences, I began to formulate some theories as to what may have been accounting for this newfound awareness. For one, the combination of sustained yoga practice, prolonged psychedelic use and an increasing openness to the very idea of multidimensionality served to catalyze an ability to perceive beyond the ordinary senses. The communities with which I'd come into contact made no attempt to conceal their similar beliefs, choosing instead to embrace a "new paradigm" of conscious living in which mystical, psychic, and spiritual experiences—terms that were often used interchangeably—were just as valid as any others.

I witnessed palpable, albeit invisible aspects of my own consciousness becoming increasingly refined. For instance, by this stage I had developed a heightened sense of energy awareness, including an intimate relationship with my chakras and *nadis*, the energy centers and nerve channels that— according to tantric yoga and new age culture—interweave to form an intricate, luminous, energy body around and within the physical body. It was rare that I could *see* the chakras with my naked eye, but I'd met several people who claimed they had such vision all the time, in addition to possessing other psychic abilities such as clairvoyance. Likewise, I concluded that my disciplined examination of dreams had served to enhance the capacities of my "dream body." Each night when I went to sleep, the part of me that was dreaming was growing stronger, well-defined, capable in-and-of itself, and more adept at navigating the laws (or lawlessness) of the dream world. During this period, I also had lucid dreams—dreams in which I knew that I was dreaming—every few days.

It wasn't difficult to deduce that *energy* was the common denominator. Almost everyone I had met while traveling to festivals was interested in learning about it, working to enhance their ability to perceive it and, in many cases, had devoted their life to raising awareness of energy both in themselves and in others. However, because we were all essentially nomadic and the Internet was still young, there were few bona fide teachers to speak of and little dialogue about the particulars of consciousness expansion. We were searching in the dark, literally.

CHAPTER 16
THE FIFTH DIMENSION

AS I JOURNEYED FURTHER into the recesses of my mind,
I began to spill the beans to just about anyone who would
listen. It seemed obtuse to discuss anything other than what
was *really* going on—namely, a wondrous, underexplored,
metaphysical exchange between each of us and the Universe in
every single moment.

Even amongst the initiated, I was met with resistance.
Stephen only gave me information on a need-to-know basis,
and it was usually cryptic and full of metaphor. When I tried to
talk about consciousness with like-minded peers, it seemed that
most people were either insecure about their own experiences,
lacked the language to express them, or felt stifled by
mainstream culture, including family, friends, co-workers, and
employers who thought it was all mumbo jumbo.

Some people felt the need to compete, claiming that they
were "higher" than others, or believing that others were higher
than them. Many people were defensive about their own
worldview, and skeptical of anyone else interested in shaking it
up. Rarely did people wish to meet me from a place of not
knowing. My parents were some of the first to feel alienated,
and vice versa. Despite having put up with my wacky stories
for a couple years, they would go blank when I'd start sharing

insights, would accuse me of proselytizing, and increasingly tuned me out.

There were a few people that *did* listen, though, and even had a lot to say about the topic. In particular, there was Brian Haas—the pianist and mastermind behind the Jacob Fred Jazz Odyssey—who I had met at High Sierra the previous summer. When he came to Portland that winter to play a show, he invited me out for breakfast the following morning.

I had come to recognize that touring musicians were an odd breed, bouncing around from city to city in a crowded, smelly van, day after day for months on end. I thought it remarkable that they could remember where they were at all. Sitting across from Brian over bowls of scrambled tofu, he exuded confidence, spoke a mile-a-minute, and was supremely focused.

"I first felt interconnected with everything when I was a kid riding the school bus and during piano recitals," he said. "I'd improvise over Bach and Mozart. The audience had no clue!" he laughed.

When I shared with him some of the weird things I'd experienced, he brimmed with excitement.

"You know what that tells me?" he said. "That you've awakened *kundalini*! You're an old soul. You've lived many lives before this one."

He abruptly straightened his spine and softened his gaze. I felt a series of quick, popping sensations in my groin.

"You're storing your seed, aren't you?" he said, raising an eyebrow.

Somehow, he had intuited that I'd been practicing *brahmacharya*—sexual celibacy, in this case—and had gone more than half-a-year without ejaculating.

"How do you know that?" I replied, dumbfounded and embarrassed.

"You better be careful with that," he fired back, disregarding my question. "I tried that in high school when I was eighteen. I got all-powerful."

He raised his arms to shoulder height, curling his biceps.

"And then I burned my brain! You don't want to end up in the hospital like I did. Better that you wait until you're thirty. Then, if you're lucky, you'll find someone special to practice with."

I nodded, still a bit taken aback.

Finally, he shared with me his top ten greatest jazz recordings of all time—each one by a pianist, naturally. As he stood to leave, my third eye began to throb.

"You see," he said, locking eyes with me again as the pulsing intensified, "we're all connecting at a faster and faster rate. We're remembering that we're one being, one mind. We're all *activating* each other, helping each other wake up."

Just like the "hundredth monkey" experiment Rob Newton had spoken of, many travelers, dreamers and adherents to the new paradigm seemed to agree that simply hanging out and sharing energy served to accelerate our individual and collective evolution. These themes became increasingly commonplace in the marketing schemes of festival organizers, clothing designers, artists and homemakers alike. When you conversed with someone who was "tapped-in" or "connected," you were resonating at the level of the Spirit, which felt meaningful and, more often than not, supremely pleasurable.

In some instances, however, connecting with another person felt like a toxic flow was entering into your system or, conversely, as if energy was draining out but not coming back in. I was especially troubled by the fact that that nobody was discussing the consequences of all this energy exchange, choosing instead to embrace a naïve idealism by believing that everything was positive, loving and pure.

My experiences repeatedly showed me otherwise. I was convinced that there was an energy lag after having an "open" encounter with another activated person. Afterward, it appeared possible to stay connected to the other party, as if by an energetic thread or cord that remained attached to and, in some cases, woven deeply into one's luminous body. Through these cords, I hypothesized, one could gain access to and transmit another's energy like radio waves, even across impossible, geographical distances. As I tested my theory, "tuning in" to other's minds and energy fields, I reasoned that it was improbable that the other party was aware of my subtle presence. Yet, on occasion I would start to feel waves of vibration emanating through my own body and would simply know that someone or something was tapping into me from afar. If I listened deeply enough, sometimes I could even deduce the faint, silent voice of the visitor identifying itself.

Alberto Montana visited me in my mind on several occasions both while awake and in dreams. I was certain that I wasn't making these visitations up, as suddenly I would feel an unwelcome force seize my being, and images that I couldn't possibly have construed on my own would flood my mind's eye like a movie. This would often happen after using cannabis, or while I lied in bed in the moments prior to falling asleep when the mind enters into a peculiar, liminal state called *hypnagogia*.

In one instance, Montana's presence arrived late at night and seemingly took over my body, demanding that I take a smoke. Curiosity won out and I submitted, only to be bombarded by the presence of several beings—other psychedelic artists—all at once. The familiar symbol of a golden triangle illuminated in the center of my forehead, and together they composed an intricately layered piece of electronic-sounding music in my awareness. They proceeded to have a telepathic conversation about me.

"You are now entering the fifth dimension!" one of them said in a robotic voice.

They made it clear that I was being recruited as a potential leader for their movement, but I lacked the courage, concentration and power to join their ranks. This only made me more determined to prove them wrong.

"He's 'last week,'" said one of the voices to Montana, who I couldn't see but felt all the while, as if he were orchestrating the entire meeting on some astral plane.

In a flash, Montana's presence emerged from the shadows, demanding quiet. I saw the image of a black cobra rear up with fangs exposed. It came down hard and struck my arm, producing a painful sting. I immediately drifted into a haze as if I'd been drugged, and fell into a dark, dreamless slumber a moment later. From that point on the image of the cobra would appear constantly in my mind. My fascination with it grew. Soon, I began to identify with it and associated it with the PAN.

Despite all this, I found it difficult to believe that Montana and his tribe of mystics were sitting around having a séance or similar ritual dedicated to me. I was not that important. I did believe, however, that there was a part of their subconscious mind's that was reaching out. Having thoroughly examined Castaneda's work, amongst others, I didn't dismiss the idea that one's consciousness can operate in several places at the same time. Was it possible that Montana's "higher self" was working autonomously in a subtle dimension in ways that he may not even have been aware of?

Over the course of a year, I became cognizant of an entire community of dreamers, many of them connected to Montana and the PAN. While I slept I frequently found myself in dream schools—crowded astral institutions where we would practice various artistic, psychic and dream techniques. Montana would often come, both in dream and in the moments upon waking— the *hypnopompic* state—to deliver advice. His voice repeatedly encouraged me to quit my job in order to focus entirely on my art and experiments.

Meanwhile, in waking life, I would meet other dreamers at parties or even on the street and we'd simply stare into each other's eyes and wait for an inner recognition. It was as if we

141

had already met on the other side and knew that something was going on behind the scenes. This was precisely what scared me the most.

My tireless efforts notwithstanding, it was impossible for me to remember every dream I'd had, nor did I feel that I was in control of the vast majority of them. On the contrary, I came to realize there was an energetic hierarchy based on the strength of an individual's mind. Those that had the ability to focus more energy seemed to influence the world around them to a greater degree. Their magnetism allowed them to manifest their own ideal reality, to *live* their dream, in which less energized beings were essentially bit players.

The Taoist sage Lao Tzu is purported to have said, "To a mind that is still, the whole universe surrenders." What he meant was, a still mind has realized that it is not separate from the vast ocean of awareness—the sea of undifferentiated energy. In merging with it, the individual can harness tremendous power. A person literally begins to overflow with energy and exudes "star" power or charisma. To a *seer*, such a person may even radiate white light or give off shockwaves. Likewise, in Tibetan *thangka* paintings and religious iconography across cultures, enlightened beings such as Buddhas, saints and even Jesus are depicted with rainbow auras or bright halos around their bodies.

We all have these energy fields around us, I deduced, but some people are so magnetized that we can't help but be attracted to them, both physically, mentally, emotionally, and spiritually—it's a law of nature. Because we're forced to yield to their superior magnetism, it slowly molds our own energy body like a river does a stone until, sometime in the future, we've actually become them—we resonate with the subtle energy of the same frequency. Consequently, when an open person decides to go with the flow, they are blown about like a leaf in the wind. En lieu of proper energetic boundaries, a sense of grounding and a concise, intentional direction, such people may be unknowingly at the mercy of more powerful beings.

Having arrived at these conclusions, a nagging fear developed. Was it possible that many of the dreamers I had met—myself included—were being programmed on a subtle, subconscious level more easily identified in the dream state? I witnessed that the more I interacted with members of the PAN, both while asleep and while awake, the more I was becoming like them via an invisible process of resonance. Beyond that, the subculture as a whole seemed to develop a grim outlook and prophesied—almost banked on—the end of days.

Montana, and who knew who or what else, appeared to be harvesting the energy of the group mind, like a queen bee forever strengthening itself and its hive via the labor of its drones. Perhaps the strangest discovery of all was that in my dreams I was routinely transported down the West Coast to a secret locale in California near Big Sur, although I could never figure out why. I wondered if there was some beacon there—a dream headquarters—where a mental magician was beaming out a signal to all of the open minds.

Things got worse before they got better. As I drifted off to sleep one evening I began to perceive a silent voice imparting to me a full-fledged fairytale.

"There once was a young man who came home to find his mother choking in the kitchen," began the voice. "He quickly ran to her aid, reached down into her throat and, after a terrible struggle, removed a large, shiny white pearl that had been lodged there. Curious as to its origin, the young man took the pearl to the sea, where he dove deep to the ocean floor. There he encountered a giant oyster. As he inspected the oyster, it opened its shell and swallowed him whole. The young man was immersed in total darkness, though gradually he lit a torch and began to explore the space around him. He soon discovered that he was not alone. There were others there exploring the darkness, just like him."

I fell asleep as the story finished but, before long, abruptly shot up in bed. I was choking violently. I could feel something the size of an egg being forced down my throat. I tried to fight it off and screamed as loud as I could.

"Get out!" I yelled in my mind.

In a flash, I woke up again. The struggle had been a false awakening—a dream within a dream. Now in my *real* bed, I appeared to be free of the intruder.

The exact sequence of events is no longer clear to me, but right around this same time, I began to receive guidance from some sort of discarnate, superconscious entity, as if it had attached itself to me. I don't know for certain if this entity was the one that told me the story of the pearl or tried to choke me, but from then on out I felt I was no longer alone. Something else was constantly present, was aware of my every thought and action, and was incessantly offering advice. For a while I thought that it was just my mind playing tricks on me or the awakening of some latent intuitive ability or higher self. However, I soon began to differentiate between its thoughts and my own. I noticed its unique style of communicating, its use of unfamiliar language and its knowledge of information, some of it precognitive, that I couldn't possibly have known.

While I found this guide to be surprisingly useful, like having a special helper that could see the future and tell me what others were thinking, between it and the premonition that I was being sucked into a psychedelic cult against my will, I was more or less on the verge of complete insanity. At the same time, I trusted my experience implicitly, even when people thought I was nuts.

CHAPTER 17
THE ROOSTER COMB

IN THE SUMMER OF 2005, I eagerly accepted an invitation to join Tristan and his camp of Oregonians at Burning Man in Black Rock City, Nevada. I had been interested in "the Burn," an annual event held the week prior to Labor Day, ever since having watched a documentary on it with Penelope in college. Excited for this initiation and with time to spare, I decided to take the scenic route through the sparse, high deserts of Eastern Oregon and, in particular, the Steens Mountains in the most remote corner of the state. I had heard that the Steens were among the more incredible, unknown destinations in the entire U.S., boasting a mile-high, sheer drop-off to the sprawling Nevada desert below.

I drove two long days beneath the scorching August sun to reach the Steens. Each mile drew me further and further away from any signs of civilization. Finally, I arrived at the mountaintop as the last bands of orange light streaked across the horizon. I had a wondrous night's sleep on the cliffside, where I dreamt with 19th century gold rushers who convinced me that they still resided in the clear blue, astral version of the same locale. In the early morning, I sat on the ridge and admired golden eagles soaring through the warm jet stream that rose up the steep rock-face from the dusty flats. Afterward, I hopped back in my car, still going strong despite the torture it had endured, and proceeded down the backside of the loop road I'd driven in on. At the very top of the hill, just before the descent, I noticed a small, white sign with a cartoon picture of a bright red chicken on it. It read: *Rooster Comb: Not recommended for low clearance vehicles or RVs.*

My car had exceptionally low clearance.

If it were really bad it would say, "prohibited," I thought.

I started down the mountain. Moments later, I watched the precarious gravel road transform into a treacherous, single-lane, dirt road laden with sharp, protruding rocks. They may as well have been landmines. There was nowhere to stop, no way to turn around, and no place to duck out of the way of oncoming traffic. Cautiously steering over and around the obstacles, I winced each time a jagged edge disappeared beneath the car's belly and lifted my body off the driver's seat as if to will the chassis higher. Panicked and sweating profusely, I felt the sun beat down upon the black leather interior and my sticky skin. Despite my agitation, I was in awe of the few glimpses I caught of the breathtaking scenery.

"Bang!" went the hull. In an instant, my luck had run out, and with it poured a thick black liquid that trailed the car some ten meters.

With nowhere to go but down, I crept on, careful not to drive clear off the mountainside or pierce the hull again. Red lights began to blink across the dashboard and the car screeched, moaned and shuddered like a wounded animal. It was then that I commenced praying, fiercely, making all sorts of promises to God and repenting for my sins. I didn't know how far away I was from intelligent life and knew there was a chance I wouldn't make it out alive.

Squeezing every last ounce of strength out of myself and the car, I managed to work it down to an area where the road leveled off. I pulled off to the side and shut down the engine. Breathing an enormous sigh of relief, yet well aware that I was by no means out of the woods, literally, I reached into the glove box and found the owner's manual. I looked up the various symbols that had lit-up the dashboard. This time the instructions were clear: *CEASE OPERATING THE VEHICLE IMMEDIATELY!*

Roughly twenty miles from the nearest state road, a hundred miles from the closest town, and in a park that drew an average of four visitors per day, I placed the keys back in the ignition and tried to start the car. It was completely dead. The engine had seized. Down but not out, I spilled onto the road like a puddle, sought shelter beneath a juniper tree and waited. Two cars passed by in the span of an hour. Both of them stopped, though neither driver offered me a lift. One suggested I follow a rough trail through the low brush to a ranger's station about a half-mile away.

"There's no telling whether anyone'll be there but it's worth a shot. That or die," he said, before speeding off to tackle the Rooster Comb for himself.

Grabbing two liters of water from the car, which was loaded with supplies for Burning Man, I took off into the woods. Twenty minutes later, I found the outpost but no rangers. I had started back when a pickup truck roared up beside me.

"What in the hell are you doing out here?" It was a forest ranger.

"Car broke down, sir," I said, struggling to keep it together.

"Rooster Comb got you, huh?"

I nodded.

"Does your phone work out here?" I said. "I can't get a signal."

"Service is spotty but we'll give it a shot. Let me take a look at her first before we start dealing with insurance companies and all that. Hop in."

We drove back to the car, which he tried to start just as I had.

"Nope. She's all messed up," he concluded after peeking under the scalding hood.

He immediately put in a call for a tow-truck from the closest town, Burns, Oregon—population three thousand—which was about two hours away.

"Wow, that's a long way to drive for a tow," I said.

"They do it all the time. You wouldn't believe how many cars get swallowed up out here," said the ranger matter-of-factly. "They really ought to change that sign."

Two hours later I was riding shotgun in a tow-truck, backtracking most of the distance I'd covered the previous day.

"Whatever you do," said the driver, "don't let 'em try to fix your car in Burns. They don't even know how to spell 'Volkswagen' out there!"

149

"Yeah, I've been down that road before," I said, recalling my car's purgatory in Colorado.

The following morning, less than twenty-four hours after the accident, I was given a loaner and was back on the road. I arrived at Burning Man on time, reunited with Tristan and his crew, and spent much of the week roaming the desert by bike with my camera. It seemed that everything I could imagine was at Burning Man, as well as everything I couldn't possibly have imagined. There were pirate ships on wheels, semi-trucks suspended in mid-air, naked people roaming free and, at the center of it all, a giant, wooden statue of a man awaiting sacrifice.

Still shell-shocked from my encounter with Alberto Montana and the bizarre events that had followed, I felt like my sanity was under constant assault.

The week went by quickly for me as I opted to sleep at night while everyone else was out partying. Instead, I dreamt my way around the *playa*, meeting total strangers and experiencing one adventure after another. Awake one afternoon, however, I managed to track down Annabelle, who I hadn't seen since my cross-country trip the previous Fall. We had mostly fallen out of touch.

"Baby!" she called out when she saw me. "I was hoping we'd find each other."

She wrapped her arms around me tightly. Her embrace was utterly familiar.

"Looks like you've got quite the set up," I said, examining her campsite. "This place is nicer than most peoples' home."

She was staying with a large group of artists that included Michael Franti, a famous musician with a well-publicized penchant for yoga.

"I'm just along for the ride," she said. "I've missed you."

"I've missed you, too."

Annabelle and I spent a few hours dancing together on the parched earth before a dust storm blanketed the city. The whipping winds blew us in opposite directions.

On the night of the Burn itself, I rode with Tristan to the massive, fiery remains of the towering effigy that had served as an axis. Without it, it was next to impossible to orient oneself on the playa.

"Happy New Year!" Tristan shouted over the roar of the inferno. "What are you ready to let go of?"

Closing my eyes, I tossed a crumpled, $20 bill into the blaze, symbolic of my discontent with the seductively materialistic, Western lifestyle.

"I've got to quit my job," I said.

"If I've learned one thing out here," said Tristan, who had already attended several burns, "it's that you don't make any major life decisions until *after* Burning Man."

His words fell on deaf ears. I was burned out, lonely, and desperate for relief.

It wasn't until November, exactly one year after I had arrived in Portland, that I realized I truly was losing my mind. Dreading another rainy winter and on the verge of a nervous breakdown, I had a long talk with my folks. I explained my concern about the psychic cult that seemed to be invading my consciousness. My parents were exceedingly worried. They urged me to move back to Massachusetts, where they had relocated full-time, and suggested I live with them until I figured out my next move.

I was on the fence until the week before Thanksgiving when Leo, my childhood friend from New York, came to visit. He had spent the better part of two years traveling in India and working with NGOs in the Himalayas. He'd returned to the States to help care for his younger brother, who was suffering from cancer at the age of twenty-one. It was a heartbreaking situation, as their mother had died from cancer only five years earlier. In need of a respite, Leo booked a flight to Oregon and we planned a camping trip to some hot springs outside Eugene.

The night he arrived in Portland I picked him up at the airport, took him back to my place, and promptly dumped all my drama on him. He was at a loss, especially as he had always been skeptical of my esoteric tales, but he kept his composure and spoke very clearly.

"Look around you," he said. "You hardly own anything! You could be out of this place in a day."

He was right. My house was not my home, it was just a place where I stored my stuff, and I had come to realize that the more I possessed, the more distracted I was by it. Leo had been living out of a backpack since his junior year in college and encouraged me to go abroad, essentially giving me a kick in the butt.

"Traveling is where it's at," he said. "It's the best thing you can do for yourself. Besides, it could all be over in a moment."

Two days later I worked my last sales job, selling one hundred-forty boxes of energy drink mix over ten hours and earning a hefty commission for my efforts. When I got paid, I put the cash in an envelope labeled "Stephen's India Fund" and gave it to my yoga teacher as an offering. He hadn't once asked for compensation for his teachings though he had referred to saving every dime he'd made to "get back to 'Ma'"—the motherland—as he put it. As Leo was planning to do the same a couple months later, this was my chance to go to India, too.

The day I left Portland, it started raining and didn't stop for thirty days. I watched the clouds descend upon the city as I hit the highway and sped off toward California. It was December 2005, and I suspected the northern routes across the country might be treacherous. I drove south through the Humboldt redwoods, camped along US 1 in Mendocino, slept on the beach outside Santa Barbara, skirted around LA, and plowed through the desert to Joshua Tree National Park. There I met owls, wolves, and fellow tourists in my dreams night after night and felt joy return to my being. From Joshua Tree, I proceeded south to the Salton Sea, which Devon had once pointed out to me on a map.

Upon further investigation, I was directed to Slab City, a seasonal squatter compound beside an old, abandoned army base. The "Slabs," I learned, played host to some of the zaniest, sun-drenched, dehydrated, and wrinkled people imaginable. During my short stay, I met a guy who had built a "salvation mountain" out of colorful paper mâché and had dedicated it to

God, and another who lived in a trailer crawling with rattlesnakes.

Onward through Flagstaff, Arizona, I pitched my tent beneath a giant saguaro cactus at a state park within earshot of I-10. In the early morning hours, I became lucid and flew out of my body, allowing an invisible force to carry me wherever it pleased. It brought me all the way back to Oregon, like a rubber band, before depositing me in a vacant room inside a hospital. I sat beside a phone, which began to ring. I picked it up. Coretta's voice answered.

"You're home," she said.

At the Great Sand Dunes in New Mexico I still hadn't shaken Montana's psychic energy, which was continually urging me to take photographs and even applauded when I composed a pleasing one. Among other things, it told me that I would soon be interacting "with thousands of *seers*" and that, one day, "the whole world will listen."

It took two tedious days to cross Texas before reaching Pass Christian, Mississippi, where Devon was holed up as a volunteer assisting the relief effort in the aftermath of Hurricane Katrina. We only spent one night together but, after a smoke beneath some oak trees, we sat facing each other with roughly ten feet between us. Out of nowhere, he emitted a tractor beam of rainbow light that drilled me in the center of my forehead.

"Gotcha!" he said enthusiastically, as the light poured forth from his mind into mine.

"What the hell is going on?" I said.

"I don't know what it is," he said, "but I know we're putting more of it on the Earth."

After a brief stop in Atlanta for Sound Tribe's New Year's Eve show, I headed south to Miami to seek refuge at my grandmother's home. I spent my free time meditating and trying to force my "guide"—the brash voice in my head that I'd decided was definitely an unwelcome, foreign entity—out of my mind. Unsure what to do, I ranted to Stephen via email.

"Suck it up!" he said, along with the suggestion to go in the ocean as much as possible to "clear [my] energy field."

After a few weeks, I still hadn't rid myself of the voice, but I did manage to sell my car, which was on its second motor after the accident at the Rooster Comb and had definitely seen better days. With a lightened load and enough money to last me a few months, I retreated for home. I hoped that my best days were yet to come.

CHAPTER 18
GANGOTRI

HAVING LEFT THE WEST COAST in a hurry, I spent the first few months of 2006 with my parents in the Berkshires. I had shipped all my equipment back East and continued to process photos, built a website to display them, and upgraded my camera gear in preparation for whatever life might throw at me. Along with the decision to quit my sales job came the conclusion that I had to give myself to my art completely.

The psychic voice I'd picked up in Portland pushed me to work harder and harder, assuring me that I would be successful if I stuck with my artistic and spiritual development. At some point, I began to question the voice's motives and read up on spiritual possession in an effort to figure out what was going on. The books I found led me to believe that an entity might be "riding" me—feeding off my energy and playing out its karma through me.

Meanwhile, Leo's brother's condition continued to worsen. Leo had returned to work in India and encouraged me to join him. Though I had been excited by the prospect during his last visit, now that I was home I was having second thoughts.

One evening I dreamt that Leo's late mother came to me in the lobby of a New York City apartment building. Her radiant image appeared through a mirror. She was dressed in a black beret and a vibrant purple shawl, like one she might have worn when she was alive. Her features were youthful and healthy. She seemed to shine through the glass.

"Thank you for sticking with him," she said.

I knew she was talking about Leo.

The experience was so palpable that I woke up in the middle of the night with tears streaming down my face, utterly certain that she had reached out to me from beyond the grave. Drifting back to sleep a few minutes later, I dreamt that Leo and I were drinking chai in a bright, airy, white-walled Indian café nestled in the side of a mountain. Outside the window were evergreens and a raging river far below.

A few days passed before I spoke with Leo over the phone and, despite a crackly connection, relayed to him my decision to meet him in India. I also told him everything I had seen in the dreams. As I described the visions, he was so quiet that I wasn't sure he was still there.

"When did you have that dream of my mom?" he asked once I'd finished.

"Last Saturday," I said.

"Last Saturday was my brother's birthday."

Ever since I had started reporting the psychic phenomena I'd witnessed, Leo had always been uneasy and hesitant to believe me. Through the silence, however, I could tell that this time he was listening.

On the fifth of May, Leo picked me up at the New Delhi airport. The heat was already sweltering at five a.m. People were everywhere, moving about in all directions like ants. The air was thick with smoke and, even at that early hour, the city clamored with life. We took refuge at a friend's home, had a huge Indian breakfast and, that afternoon, boarded a crowded train for the northern city of Dehradun, where Leo was based. From there, we traveled to a rural, mountainous region of Uttaranchal province to assist with the inauguration of a small children's school tucked away in a remote village accessible only by half-a-day's walk. The transition from place to place was so abrupt, it was difficult to fathom that I had left the States less than three days prior.

After numerous ceremonies and a long afternoon spent singing and dancing with the kids, I positioned a narrow piece of tarp in the center of the school's concrete patio and lied down for a nap. The smoke of fire hearths wafted through the otherwise clear blue sky, which slowly faded behind my weary eyelids. Moments later, I dreamt that I was resting in that exact spot on the patio when a large cow approached me. It paused briefly before magically transforming into an obscure childhood friend that I hadn't seen in twenty years. Her name was Maya, which in Sanskrit means "illusion."

"If you continue to lie here you will receive an infection," said the cow-woman matter-of-factly.

I woke up startled and looked over at Leo, who was sitting in an old wooden rocking chair and reading *The New Yorker*. I told him what I'd seen. He raised a skeptical eyebrow from behind the tattered magazine.

"If I believed everything I saw in my dreams," he said, "the world would be a terrible place."

Too lazy and indifferent to move, I quickly fell back asleep.

The next morning, we set out on a hike to the top of a nearby mountain overlooking the village. About halfway up the trail I became violently ill and doubled over with stomach pain. As I writhed on the forest floor, Leo was stunned, and I was angry with myself for not having listened to the overt warning of the previous afternoon. Consequently, we cut our trip short. Hours later, I used my last ounce of strength to hop onto the top of a school bus working its way down to Dehradun. About half way through the eight-hour journey, we stopped at a well-lit *dhaba*—an Indian café—wedged into the side of a mountain with a spectacular view of the holy Yamuna River at the base of the ravine. Bollywood music videos blared from a television screen in the corner. We ordered *aloo parathas*—thick, fried, doughy pancakes stuffed with potatoes. Leo went to the bathroom and, picking my droopy head up from the table, I looked out the open window at the ridge, lined with evergreens, and the tiny whitecaps far below. It suddenly dawned on me that I had already visited this place. Without a doubt, it was the café from my dream.

Back in Dehradun, Leo caught the stomach bug from me and suffered similarly. Two weeks later, when we had finally recovered, we set out for the headwaters of the holy *Ganga*—the river Ganges—and the high peaks of the Himalayas beyond. It took two full days of travel to reach Gangotri, a revered pilgrimage site and the last town prior to the raw wilderness. During the final leg of our journey, I once again found myself flying along jagged, cliffside, switchback roads overlooking a gargantuan drop below. Unlike my disaster at the Rooster Comb, this time I clung to the rusty, steel handle bars of a rickety, over-crowded Jeep with no doors. The valley was lined with the carcasses of several fallen buses, trucks and vehicles just like ours. It made sense to me that in a country of one billion people, tragic accidents were commonplace, but that didn't help alleviate my fear.

At each curve, I ground my teeth and silently bid farewell to my loved ones. The driver was a disheveled man in his eighties who drove faster than his age and nearly missed colliding with a number of cars, let alone swerving off the perilous road out of sheer recklessness. At one point my entire body shook with anxiety. A stranger sitting in the front seat looked back at me.

"Do not be afraid," he said softly, his gleaming brown eyes coating me with warmth. "Life is over only for an instant."

Somehow his words relieved my plight and extinguished much of my fear, though not all of it. It wasn't until well after I had returned home to States that I realized how much fear I had been carrying with me. If only I'd known his secret all along.

After arriving safely in Gangotri, Leo and I hiked for several days into the foothills of Mount Shivling, the iconic birthplace of Hinduism. Leaping over narrow streams that ultimately feed the most sacred river in India, we arrived at Tapovan, an alpine meadow situated sixteen thousand feet above sea level. Because the air was much thinner there, it took a couple days to acclimate so that when we stood up our heads wouldn't spin. Apart from a handful of travelers who had also braved the arduous journey were a couple of ascetics, *Maharaji* (great king) and *Mataji* (great mother), who resided in a small cave at the far end of the plateau. Supposedly the pair lived in Tapovan, roughly twenty kilometers trek from the nearest market, for nine months out of the year. They hosted travelers in their hermitage, asking only for a small donation. While he kept a respectful distance by day, at night I dreamt that Maharaji and I walked the banks of the river side-by-side.

"We make friends with just about everyone that comes up here," he said in the dream.

I'd yet to see Mataji in either a waking or dreaming state, however, as she rarely left the cave and was revered by all.

At dusk the following evening, Leo and I were invited to join Maharaji for rice, *dal* (lentils) and *chapati* (flatbread), along with three orange-robed *sadhus*—Hindu holy men—at the foot of their abode. Afterward, one of the sadhus we had befriended asked me to follow him inside. His name was Sushantmuni, which means "peaceful mind." Leo walked back to our tent as I crawled into the dimly lit cavern and crouched down amongst several men lying on the floor. They were packed-in tightly and covered with thick, woolen blankets. Sushantmuni, a thin man roughly my age with long black hair, took a seat in a dark corner and beckoned me closer.

"This is Mataji," he said with admiration, motioning to a small, round woman with wide eyes who sat down beside him. As we made eye contact, the whole room seemed to shudder with energy, as if an inaudible rhythm had suddenly intensified.

161

My mind scrambled for a foothold. My eyes darted around the room. I could barely see Sushantmuni's silhouette in the shadows, and Mataji had begun to rock back and forth in her seat. A million thoughts flooded my brain at once. Mataji, who didn't speak a word, recaptured my gaze. In an instant, my attempt to figure out what was going on was vanquished by a single, undeniable intuition: *Mataji is pure love.*

As the thought surfaced, I felt a tremendous expansion in my chest and outpouring of love toward her that was met in full. She beamed an enormous smile.

"You see," spoke Sushantmuni in a soft, soothing voice, "I am just a soul."

Any trace of his body had vanished in the candle-lit darkness.

"You are also a soul, and you understand this though you do not yet *know* it."

I nodded and thought to ask him about the profound love I was feeling.

"Yes, there is love," he said, before I could utter a word. "But it is not the same as the love between me and my *satguru* (true master). That love has *adhikara*."

Though I had never before heard that word—*adhikara*—I knew exactly what he meant. It was the love between teacher and student built over time and based upon shared experience, trust, respect and profound admiration.

*   *   *

The next day, Leo and I hiked to a small, turquoise lake above the meadow to scope out a route across the treacherous glacier beyond Tapovan. It was our good fortune to meet an old Nepali Sherpa who was staying nearby and happened to be enjoying the lake that morning. While he didn't speak much English, he conveyed that he had successfully made the journey across the glacier several times. He pointed to a number of large boulders.

"You go there, ok?"

We nodded.

Next, he motioned to an ominous, black slope, emphasizing the direction by waving his arm.

"You no go there," he warned. "There, very bad!"

He made a whistling sound between his teeth, mimicking the sound of a sliding object, and made a diving motion with his hand. Leo and I smiled in recognition, bobbing our heads side-to-side as is the Indian custom. The Sherpa began to chuckle, though clearly this was no laughing matter.

Hours later, Leo and I danced our way across a ravine of massive, shifting rocks, dodging patches of ice and deep crevasses. Finally, we ascended the opposite side of the mountain. Upon reaching solid ground, we threw down our heavy packs and hooted and hollered in celebration, startling a herd of ibex that had gathered nearby to inspect their strange, new neighbors. Drenched to the bone with sweat, we gave each other a huge, exhausted hug.

"We made it," said Leo.

We were alone at the top of the world.

Over the next few days we sat beside the crystalline stream that sliced through the stark plateau. We made up songs to sing and, at times, laughed so hard we cried. Rather than recapturing the glory days of our friendship, which had spanned fifteen years, we forged a new bond built upon our *yatra*—our pilgrimage.

Individually, we both took time to pray for Leo's brother, though in one such session I imagined him looking back at me with disgust. Returning from my perch among the rocks, I took a deep breath and spoke to Leo.

"I don't think he wants to be healed," I said.

"I know," Leo replied. "I know."

CHAPTER 19
THE SWAMI

AS LEO AND I HIKED TOGETHER, the mountains taught us an important lesson: we had merely been seeking peace and quiet all along. The moment I realized that, it occurred to me that I could've achieved the same goal in my own backyard.

Upon returning to Dehradun, Leo went back to work and I ventured off to the fabled city of Rishikesh. I rented a room on a rooftop overlooking the holy Ganga for one hundred twenty-five rupees—or, $2.50 a night. Prior to leaving Portland, Stephen had specifically advised me to find such a place so that I could deepen my yoga practice without distraction.

"When I'm in India I wake up at 5 a.m. for *sadhana*," he'd said, "and by 10 it's chai and *chillums*"—tea and hashish—"for the rest of the day."

On most mornings I slept until 7 or 8 a.m., then practiced yoga for roughly two hours before descending the steep hill to purchase bananas, mangoes and fresh yogurt served ice cold. My routine was so consistent that one morning I even dreamt of flying down the hill before being consumed by a bright red mandala. Upon waking up and meandering to the market a couple hours later, I saw the exact same design on a bed sheet that had been left out to dry along the corridor.

Afternoons were typically spent exploring back alleys, taking photos and, in many instances, composing images in my mind and waiting patiently for a decisive moment. For example, I would find an interesting juxtaposition of colors and shapes, such as on an exotic spice display, and would wait for a woman with bright bangles on her arm to reach for the cardamom, thereby bringing the image to life. More often than not, the strategy worked. Occasionally I would come to a dead end in the road only to be invited into someone's home for chai, which would lead to a wonderful portrait, a heart-warming story or a valuable lesson. I began to truly embrace the idea that if I turned off my thinking mind and followed my intuition—my internal, vibrational compass—there were no wrong turns.

Within Rishikesh, I stayed in an area called Lakshman Jhula, a small enclave surrounding a majestic yet overly crowded, monkey-infested suspension bridge. There I had a chance encounter at a music shop with a young Indian man named Nishel. He had a soothing disposition.

"I think it's because I play didgeridoo," he said, referring to the indigenous Australian wind instrument that requires circular breathing to create a continuous, droning sound. "I get really 'zen' when I'm on the *didg*."

"Where do you practice?" I said. "I'd really like to learn to play *tabla*"—Indian hand drums—"while I'm here."

"There's a little ashram beside Ram Jhula," which was another area surrounding an equally spectacular and treacherous suspension bridge a few kilometers south. "Ask for Swami Gopeshwarananda. He is a great master."

The next day I walked to Ram Jhula, where the Beatles had famously sought enlightenment, in the oppressive midday heat. After a tough search, I found the ashram and met the Swami. A thin man in his mid-50s, he had a shiny, bald head, terribly stained teeth and impeccable posture. As he was busy reading the newspaper, he asked me to return the following afternoon but only if I was prepared to commit to regular lessons, which I was.

For our first formal practice, he led me into his small music room, a shabby, dimly lit, square chamber with dirty walls. The tattered, blue carpet was littered with broken or rotting instruments. He had a beautiful set of *tablas*, however, that he placed on the floor before me and knocked around with a small hammer.

"Sit up tall so that you can achieve the right pitch!" he demanded, startling me.

Three tedious hours later, I had realized there was no way I was going to master this instrument in the month I'd planned to spend in town. But, I found his company so enjoyable that I kept my word and agreed to come three times a week.

After a couple sessions he seemed pleased with my progress and, in an effort to encourage me to stick with it, lent me the drums, one large and one small, to practice on. I was deeply moved by his gesture and wanted so badly to honor him that I actually devoted five or six hours a day to it until I noticed it was cutting into the time I had reserved for photo walks. When I next visited him, I intended to tell him that I simply couldn't continue at the level he deserved from a student. Before I could speak, he began to talk to me about his guru, Swami Chitananda, and told me stories of all the magical things he had witnessed through the years while living in forest ashrams and chanting devotional *raags*. I shared some of my own experiences, particularly with regard to synchronicities, and mentioned that I had even begun to meet his other Western students around town with uncanny frequency.

"Ha! This is no big deal, Maharaji," he said with a booming laugh. "I have witnessed thousands of such occurrences. I have seen my guru meditate with the intention of drawing a man to the ashram from thousands of kilometers away. Two days later this man has arrived gasping for breath and not even knowing why he has come!" He laughed again, rattling the instruments in the room.

When I told him about Alberto Montana and how I'd burst into light, he grew very quiet.

"This is *samadhi*," he said, sincerely. "Realization. That man was your teacher! May I ask you, Maharaji"—he frequently referred to me this way and took great pleasure in inflating my ego—"how long did you remain in this place?"

"A few seconds, I think."

"Mmhmm," he said, nodding. "I have met several Westerners that have had this experience. You see, you are getting to know the Great Spirit!"

"You know what I'm talking about?" I was elated.

"Of course, I know!" he said again, his demeanor shifting erratically as he fed off and fueled my excitement. "You see, Maharaji," he winked, "the Spirit *jokes* with me."

168

From that day forth, when I came to visit the Swami we would go over my lessons but, sooner or later, would start talking, generally about one aspect of consciousness or another. We often wouldn't stop until nightfall. Every so often something we'd cover would inspire him to tell a story from the Vedas or the Mahabharata, the ancient texts of Hinduism. He'd begin to speak of the great heroes Ram or Arjuna but would often stop abruptly.

"This really interests you, Maharaji?" he'd ask.

"Absolutely!" I'd respond each and every time, riveted as he shared one sacred story after another.

In time, the Swami revealed that he was also remarkably in tune with how I was feeling from day to day.

"Your energy is full power," he'd proclaim upon glancing at me.

Then, one day, he looked concerned.

"Today, Maharaji, your energy has gone down," he said. "Illness is coming."

He quickly disappeared into a side room. I heard pots and pans clanging as he sang and, occasionally, cursed to himself. Several minutes later, he returned with a "special chai" made with some goopy, brown concoction he had brewed up. He claimed to have been a successful Ayurvedic doctor—a doctor of traditional Indian medicine—many years earlier, and even gave me an extensive list of naturopathic remedies that he assured me would heal my back pain, though, regrettably, I never went through the trouble of collecting them.

I was certain he could read my thoughts at any given moment, as he frequently addressed them before I'd had a chance to speak. Above all else, I left our sessions feeling rejuvenated and clear, as if some of his magic dust had rubbed off on me. I felt overwhelmingly comfortable around him, and the only topic I hadn't had the courage to discuss with him was brahmacharya—celibacy—which I'd read was a necessary component on the path to enlightenment.

One day when I arrived he said, "You should go visit Swami Sahajatmananda at Sivananda ashram. He is a Westerner also. You must tell him I sent you. I think you will like him. He is a great man."

Adhering to his wishes, I wandered up the hill to the famed ashram and found my way to the quarters of the Swami in question. He invited me in and asked me to sit down.

"Who sent you?" he asked curiously.

"Swami Gopeshwarananda from down the hill."

"Gopeshwarananda, Gopeshwara…" he repeated, scratching his head as he tried to remember. "Oh yes! Gopeshwarananda, the beautiful *kirtania*"—a leader of *kirtans* or singing rituals.

I nodded.

"Well," he said, "what do you want?"

"Nothing," I replied. "He just requested that I meet you."

There was a long silence as the elderly Swami, who wore the bright orange robes of a renunciate and reclined on a tan couch, appeared to enter into a trance. The room grew exceptionally still, and I felt his tremendous presence subsume

170

my entire body. It was accompanied by the unpleasant sensation of being energetically constricted—my chakras were being squeezed! I realized that he had engulfed me in his field of awareness in order to read my mind. As the intensity reached its apex, I silently projected the thought, *Read whatever you like—I have nothing to hide.* Suddenly, the immense pressure subsided and the Swami, who had been gazing off into the distance, turned to face me. He looked relieved.

"I can't tell you what a pleasure it is to have you here," he said. "People are always coming because they want something or are in search of some favor. It appears you are fairly empty. And please, call me Swami 'Saj.'"

With that, Swami Saj began to tell me all about his journey, which involved abandoning a successful job in Canada following a chance meeting with Swami Chitananda, his satguru, who had helped him discover his "true self." I didn't entirely understand what he meant by this, but I didn't dare interrupt him either.

"After my awakening," he continued, "I donated all my money to the ashram and moved to Rishikesh permanently. I've remained here as a monk, meditation teacher, and spiritual guide ever since."

"Do you ever wonder what life might have been like had you not given it all up?"

"Of course," he responded, "but I don't dwell on the past. You see, the spiritual life is a beautiful one full of twists and turns. It may seem like you're going one way, but actually you're heading in the complete opposite direction without even knowing it."

His smile broadened, and his genuine, blue eyes twinkled in the late afternoon sun streaking through a side window.

"Have you ever heard the tale of footprints in the sand?" he said.

"No."

"One night a man had a dream. He dreamt he was walking along the beach with God, and across the sky flashed scenes from his life. With each scene, he noticed two sets of footprints in the sand. One belonged to him and the other to God. When the last scene of his life flashed before him, he looked back at the footprints and noticed that many times along the journey of his life there was only one set. He also noticed that it happened at the very lowest and saddest times of his life. Confused, he spoke to God: 'You said that once I placed my faith in you, you'd walk with me always. But I've noticed that during the most troublesome times of my life, there is only one set of footprints. I don't understand why you deserted me when I needed you most.' To that, God replied, 'My precious, precious son, I love you and I would never leave you. During your times of trial and suffering, when you see only one set of footprints, it was then that I carried you.'"

"So you see, my son," said the Swami, "*always* have faith."

He paused to let the words sink in.

"But," he laughed, "don't be surprised if the Spirit sends you back to New York to get a job."

CHAPTER 20
BEDNI BUGYAL

WHILE HIKING IN GANGOTRI with Leo the previous
month, we had met an adventurous, Indian accountant from
Kolkata. He had told us about a trip he had taken to an off-beat
locale called Bedni Bugyal, an alpine meadow perched high in
the Himalayas.

"There are one thousand lotus flowers growing there," he'd
said.

"A thousand? Get outta here," Leo had said.

"Good sir!" the accountant had replied. "Why do you
question my integrity? I am an honest man! This is one of
India's last Shangri-La's. I swear to you, it is a paradise.
Everywhere is the lotus. When you arrive there, you will see it
with your own eyes!"

After my meeting with Swami Saj in Rishikesh one
evening, I attended a small gathering of travelers at a nearby
café. Amidst the ecstasy of *gulab jamun*—a delicious, sugary
pastry similar to a doughnut hole—I shared my plans to set out
in search of the legendary meadow. A young, Israeli woman
with dark hair named Amina perked up as I spoke of the
lotuses. Despite our having just met, she asked if she could join
me.

"Sure," I replied.

Two days later, we packed our bags and caught a bus headed toward a scarcely visited area of Uttaranchal. It was mid-July, the monsoon had begun, and the skies threatened to burst with rain at a moment's notice. After ten, tedious hours, the bus attendant manning the back door roused us from our drooling torpor.

"Chalo! Chalo! Chalo! Chalo!" he yelled. *"Let's go!"*

Peeling ourselves off the sticky, vinyl seats, we grabbed our packs and spilled onto the road near a taxi stand in the center of a dusty village. From there we caught a shared Jeep destined for the trailhead, but three hours into the ride we were halted by a boulder that had landed in the road—a common sight along the rocky, Himalayan switchbacks. As the giant stone had recently fallen, the local men had yet to descend from their huts with small hammers to chip away at it, which meant it could be days before the path would be cleared. So, from there we set out on foot, hiking five, lofty kilometers in the dark before arriving at a village with one abandoned restaurant. Fortunately, a kind man welcomed us in his home and fixed us some freshly laid eggs and rice for dinner.

At sunrise, Amina and I continued our hike toward Wan, a small village situated at the base of the mountain below Bedni Bugyal. We reached the lush homestead eight hours later and pitched our tents in a grove of thick, fir trees. As we weren't pressed for time, we took a superfluous, but appreciated, rest day at twenty-five hundred meters elevation to dry our boots, stretch our bodies and enjoy the crisp, mountain air.

I was surprised when Amina began to hint that she'd had enough of our adventure and was ready to quit prior to our final push to the Bugyal. During our short time together, we had engaged in some gentle bickering over big questions like free will and the meaning of life.

"We are failing to meet each other," she said, after she had tried in vain to persuade me that it was inhumane to eat fish.

I convinced her to stay after some guided yoga practice in the soft, green grass and even praised her undercooked dinner in an effort to salvage our alliance. Still, she threw in the towel as we broke down camp the following morning. Officially, she had become preoccupied with a pressing need to visit her guru in Benares, a town some three days away by foot, bus, and train. I'd noticed that she had also grossly overpacked, and the mountain loomed large.

"Don't worry, you're not alone," she said as she traipsed down the hillside. "It's India, a land of one billion!"

At first, I was disturbed by her rash decision to desert me in the wilderness. However, soon I realized, with joy, that I was free to move through the world as I pleased, and in full possession of all necessary resources. She had left me with our tent, stove, food, and cooking utensils. I set out to discover what laid waiting in the heights.

Perhaps Amina had foreseen the immense challenge of the final ascent to the Bugyal. The ten-kilometer trek up from the rolling emerald hills of Wan was exhausting. My back and shoulders ached, my legs burned, and my clothing was soaked with sweat. But, at each turn I was inspired by birdsong

175

echoing from the path-side brush and carpets of pink, yellow and violet wildflowers that emerged from the dripping forest and sprawled across the steep mountainside like spilled candy.

A driving rain notwithstanding, I reached Bedni at dusk and was rewarded with a spectacular sight: thin strokes of bright red snapdragons racing across a cascading jade canvas, blending softly with the dim, parting clouds. The Bengali banker had been telling the truth, at least in part. There were no lotuses, but it was paradise. The mayor of Wan, who had introduced himself the previous morning down below, was even there to greet me. He wore a tweed jacket, smoked a pipe and carried a green umbrella, which he twirled overhead. There was mutual recognition between us that we were witnessing something special.

"Arriving?" I asked, hopefully.

"Going," he replied, bobbing his head side-to-side before continuing down the stone path toward the jungle.

At dawn I was visited by a pair of identical sheepdogs, differing only in the color of their coats—one black and one gold. The soothing chimes of small bells hanging from their collars gently roused me from my slumber. Peeking out the tent window, I beheld the cloudy sky ablaze with red and purple hues. I drifted back to sleep and rose again a few hours later once the dense fog, which followed the previous night's downpour, gave way to a bright, sunlit morning.

Amazed by this unforeseen stroke of luck in the depths of the monsoon, I gathered my belongings and laid them out to dry against a horizon scattered with clandestine, snow-capped peaks. A basking troupe of jingling, smoke-black water buffaloes with silver streaks defining the creases of their bulbous hip bones chewed cud while meandering across the lush green fields. In the distance, a family of wild horses enjoyed their breakfast, exchanging glances between me and the steaming Bugyal. The land was teeming with life in all shapes and sizes, coexisting and undisturbed by anything at all.

Balwant Khatri, the only other person on the Bugyal, became a fast friend. Absent throughout most of the day, having hiked higher into the mountains to take advantage of the exceptional weather, he emerged from the afternoon mist in a green, wool sweater. A short man with thick, black hair, soft eyes and brown skin, he introduced himself as "B.K.," the official "Forest Guard" of the Bugyal. He visited my tent and smiled at me. He had come to collect more money. I'd already stayed three nights by then but had only paid for two. However, upon his arrival we began to share in the serenity of the present moment. My body was flooded with an overwhelming sense of peace and the feeling of becoming one with the meadow, harmonizing with it. I offered him a chocolate bar and together we walked to a nearby creek to pick wild berries.

When I spotted the ripe fruit, he enthusiastically exclaimed, "*buli!*" and proceeded to point out "*buki!*"—a parsley-like herb abundant in the grass—"*golas*" (horses), "*cowwas*" (cows), "*buckri*" (goats), "*dotas*" (dogs), "*benj*" (buffaloes), "*golgols*" (flowers), and a few more objects which he named in Hindi. I marveled at how slowly he moved, and how gently he brushed his callused hands over the plants. It seemed as if he lived outside of time.

B.K. invited me into his hut for tea, and I observed his sparse accommodations: sacks of rice, dal, and *aloo* (potatoes) hanging from the walls; whole-wheat flour for chapatis; *chinni* (sugar); a half-full bottle of turquoise kerosene; an extra sweater strewn upon a sole rafter; some boards stacked on the floor for sitting; three foam sleeping pads with a blanket between them; and, ample firewood scattered about. The hut let in very little light, and the darkness accentuated the bright fire he kindled to prepare his brew. We managed to maintain our bilingual conversation for nearly forty minutes, speaking mostly of distances between landmarks and frequently resorting to elaborate hand gestures in order to illustrate a point. The word "*ki-lo-me-ter*," as he said it, meant much more than a numerical measurement—it was a rich, meaningful experience. When we finished the tea, we parted ways like two appreciative neighbors, thoroughly embracing the blessing of our solitude yet grateful the other was nearby.

That evening I was humbled by pounding rains that arrived and receded in a flash, giving way to a supernatural dusk. The fog lifted over the northern mountains, leaving in its wake a thin film of cotton melting between shades of rust, pink, and ethereal bluish hues that grew deeper and darker, dancing against the twilight. The sounds of a shepherd guiding his flock up the hillside toward illuminated pastures, the enchanting smell of saturated flowers, the rustle of cascading streams, and the rhythmic clang of distant cow bells all contributed to the impenetrable calm.

I left Bedni after breakfast and headed over the southern hills before linking up with a path that I thought led to Ali Bugyal, a slightly higher plateau, before descending to the village of Didana at the bottom of the valley. Working my way into the forest, I was immediately confronted with the need to choose between multiple trails leading down the mountain. Figuring that all roads led to home and that I would soon encounter the well-established "*rasta acha*"—the "good way"—that B.K. had described to me, I weaved through the trees along muddy, narrow, crisscrossing paths. Within a few minutes, I found myself treading on dangerous terrain but lacked the option to turn back as the slope was too steep.

Forging ahead in pursuit of the sound of running water echoing from below, eventually I came to a cascading brook, which I tracked as best I could. However, the route quickly became treacherous, laden with sudden cliffs, waterfalls, slippery rocks, and fervent rapids. Panic steadily crept in as thunder rumbled through the thick forest.

In an effort to continue, I was forced to leap across the stream several times and to climb higher into the surrounding brush to skirt sheer drop-offs. I bushwhacked through bamboo groves, plowed through lush sheets of purple wildflowers three meters tall, and slid haphazardly along slick game trails, which I followed whenever they appeared. I grabbed hold of trees, swung from branches, and repeatedly dug my nails into rocks and the soaked, unforgiving earth.

The serene, unspoiled beauty of the wilderness, the struggle to maintain life, and the sheer frustration of the titanic, Himalayan abyss revealed my vulnerability, and were both my demons and saviors. At times, I felt as if I was wrapped tightly in Nature's warm blanket—as if God was carrying me. At other times, I felt lost and destined to die there.

I was certain the stream would lead to civilization but, as I began to get tired, I feared it might destroy me first. I opted to climb higher into the mountain to search for signs of a trail, following animal tracks to a patch of fresh cow dung. Never before had I been so excited to see a big pile of crap and, sure enough, moments later I spied a herd of enormous, black buffalo foraging in the brush along the slope. I stopped there, thoroughly fatigued. With nothing left to lose, I cried out in despair like a wounded animal.

"Hello, *Namaste*, Help!" I hollered, along with various other hoots and howls of distress.

My heart leaped when I heard a faint response, prompting me to remain in the general area for nearly two hours, calling out every minute or so and with much greater intensity when someone called back. The occasional sound of a villager on a distant hillside lifted my spirits and gave me faith that help was on its way. Gradually, the sounds disappeared, and I was alone again.

With precious daylight slipping away, I became disoriented. The shadowy forest seemed to be caving in on me. My backpack, saturated with sweat and rainwater, felt like an intolerable burden. I had grown frail and my mind raced. When the buffalo began to migrate, I began to follow them up the hillside, but a large bull at the back of the herd stared me down and stamped his hoof, threatening to charge. When the villager's responses had ceased altogether, draining what little remained of the hope I'd been storing, I started up yet another makeshift trail. I felt as if I were walking toward infinity.

I had barely begun my latest ascent when, seemingly from out of nowhere, two men appeared. Each of them toted umbrellas and a burlap sack over their shoulders. Seeing their tattered attire, scarred flesh, missing front teeth and bare feet, I grew anxious and afraid. They recognized my plight and motioned for me to come with them. Gripped with panic and paranoia, I followed them through the forest. They soon split up, one man intimating to the other that he was heading elsewhere to round up his cattle. Alone with a stranger in the unforgiving jungle, unparalleled waves of fear began to course through me. Shuddering with dread, I concealed my pocket knife in my palm in case he lunged at me.

We slogged higher and higher into the mountain before arriving at a small, earthen hut. The hut was positioned beside several others identical to it, all of them perched on an outcropping above the tree line. He invited me in, offered me chai and allowed me a few moments respite in his small, dank abode. Defeated, I sunk into the floor and began to drift off when, without warning, a petite, shadowy figure leaped out from over my left shoulder. My whole body jerked awake, terrified.

To my great relief, when the phantom landed I saw that it was his wife, an elderly woman beaming a radiant, toothless smile. Her bright brown eyes instantly diffused my anxiety and put me at ease. My savior was a family man. A pretty, young woman, presumably their daughter, arrived moments later and scrutinized me, giggling. More comfortable now, I thought to ask to stay but as I finished my tea, the man abruptly ushered me out and showed me the route to Didana.

"*Bahoot beria rasta*," he said, pointing to the *most excellent way.*

It was 5:30 p.m. with darkness encroaching when he insisted I start toward the village rather than waiting until the morning to descend the precarious stone stairwell another four kilometers. My legs wobbled all the way down. The sky turned pitch black. I was wet, freezing, and without a clue as to where I would sleep. I arrived at Didana. I noticed a wire-thin man in his early thirties standing outside the door of a mud hut and cradling his infant daughter tightly in his arms. He waved me inside his one-room dwelling with dirt walls and a fine, thatched roof. His name was Aan Singh, I learned. His wife, and his father, a village elder, offered me chai and a seat beside their small fire hearth. They prepared a huge meal of rice, dal, and chapatis, shared a *beedi* (a clove cigarette), and invited me to stay the night on the tarp-covered floor.

In the morning, I enjoyed a lazy breakfast with Aan and some of his relatives, drinking tea by the hearth while discussing trekking routes and the area's potential for ecotourism. Afterward, I donned my soggy clothing, bid them farewell and headed out in the rain toward Kuling, a small village on the opposite side of a river that divides two mountains. My torn, weathered soles took the worst of this final hike along the slippery, rock-studded path. As I walked, I vowed to take a long break from backpacking, and fantasized about luxuries like a hot shower, dry clothes, the internet, and a cup of strong, dark coffee. Upon reaching a narrow suspension bridge that crossed the river, I looked north into the mountains that had nearly claimed me and spotted a magnificent, hundred-meter waterfall emerging from the lush wall of mossy crags. The thought of what might have been had I encountered such a drop the previous day caused my heart to skip a beat.

Finally reaching Lohajung, my bones aching and heavy with exhaustion, I relished two buckets of steamy bathwater and a full night's rest at an old, stonewall inn. In the wee hours of the morning, I boarded a minibus bound for Rishikesh. Packed tightly alongside fourteen faceless men, I gazed out the windshield at the blinding rain and interminable fog. The driver's visibility was limited to roughly five feet. Water entered in through the cracks in the windows and dripped along my neck and wrist. As we rolled slowly down razor-edged switchbacks, eerie devotional music praising Shiva, the venerable God of death and destruction, blared from a crackling, dilapidated dashboard stereo. The unease I experienced easily matched the apprehension I'd felt while lost in the mountains.

Here, I thought, *one might expect a group of anonymous men on a small bus to fall off the face of the earth.* The air was thick with tension, and it was painfully obvious that the other travelers shared my sentiments.

About an hour after we had set out, the faintest traces of light could be seen parting the clouds. Shortly thereafter, we stopped alongside the road to pick up a mother and her young daughter, who sat side-by-side at the front of the bus. As they joined us, a prodigious sigh of relief echoed through the vehicle. The presence of two women instantly shifted the mood for the better. The skies cleared, bodies went slack, and we all settled-in for the long journey back to Ganga.

CHAPTER 21
BENARES

UPON RETURNING TO RISHIKESH, I fell violently ill and spent several days locked away in my hotel room. When I recovered, I decided it was time to move on. Prior to departing, however, I paid a final visit to Swami Gopeshwarananda, who knew I had gone hiking but didn't know if and when I'd return.

"I thought you had vanished, Maharaji!" he exclaimed.

He pinched my forearm to make sure I was real.

"I wish you had told me your travel dates!" he said. "I would have come with you. I have always wanted to visit such places."

He was busy with another student, a young Indian singer whom he barked at incessantly—apparently the "Great King" stuff was reserved for the tourists. Rather than disturb them, I thanked him profusely for his tutelage and companionship, and offered him a small pair of audio speakers I had decided to part with. He had often complained about not having a decent sound system for his recitals and his face lit up when he saw them.

"How did you know tonight is the recital!?" he asked.

"Recital? I didn't know."

"I was just saying that we need some speakers and here they have appeared. *Aum Namah Shivaya!* Blessed is the great Spirit!"

"I'm glad you like them," I said, "and I hope they do the trick. Swami, before I go I have one favor to ask in return."

"What is that?" he said.

"May I take your portrait?"

I had been waiting patiently for the right moment to ask him. I idolized him and had imagined a beautiful image worthy of his grandeur, but I didn't want to offend him or be shot down.

"Let us go!" he said, raising a bony index finger in the air. We slipped outside and, as the Swami was constantly in motion and never stood still, quickly produced a series of images that ranked among my favorites. After exchanging deep bows of gratitude, he looked me dead in the eyes.

"There is still one more thing, isn't there, Maharaji?"

"What?"

"Celibacy!" He grinned from ear to ear.

"How did you know?" I said. I couldn't believe it.

"Do not take a girlfriend, Maharaji." He shook his finger at me in half-jest, as if he knew full well I wasn't quite ready for that sort of vow.

That same night I departed for the holy city of Varanasi, also known as Benares, Stephen's home away from home where I would spend my last few weeks in India. It was already August. While riding an overnight train, I imagined Sammy, the barefooted, starry-eyed wayfarer I had met at the Fishbowl in Vancouver. I finally understood what he had meant when he'd said, "traveling is a state of mind." All that seemed to matter was attending to my basic needs and staying open to any and all opportunities for new experiences. Fortunately, every street corner in the filthy, over-crowded, glorious city on the sacred Ganges was filled with surprises.

In Benares, giant cows lumbered through the narrow streets and vendors called out from every direction hawking their wares, from Hindu iconography and Bollywood DVDs to delectable sweets like gulab jamun and *bhang lassi*, a notorious yogurt shake mixed with a powerful dose of cannabis. Originally intended for holy men, who were legally permitted to use the plant for spiritual purposes, bhang was typically sold to unwary foreigners who would spend the afternoon hallucinating, speaking in tongues, and stumbling through the already carnival-like atmosphere.

Fortune tellers and astrologers promising miraculous visions and spontaneous healing beckoned passersby from shadowy, second-story windows. Exotic smells—not all of them pleasant, given the preponderance of free-roaming beasts—filled the air; and, backpackers young and old played dress-up in elven-inspired outfits, which any number of tailors would custom-make for a few hundred rupees. There were silk shops galore, some of them gaudy and grandiloquent; European bakeries every few blocks; and poor, half-naked sadhus adorned in prayer beads, sitting cross-legged in smoky doorways with their eyes bleary and begging bowls extended.

Along the river were the *ghats*—large stairwells leading down to the water where people from all walks of life performed *puja* (ritual prayer), bathed, and even drank from the river to wash away their bad karma. Each ghat had a different feel to it and some were busier than others. None was more ominous than Manikarnika, the "burning" ghat, where families dragged their recently deceased loved ones to be cremated and tossed into Ganga. In Portland, Stephen had shown me photos of himself cleaning an ancient stone temple just beside Manikarnika, where he said the funeral pyres had been burning continuously for fifteen hundred years. He had also told me stories about an arcane sect of yogis called *aghori*. Aghori were sorcerers known for sitting beside bodies as they burned, and occasionally eating their limbs to pay homage to Kali, the Goddess of destruction.

When I went to see the burning ghats for myself, I didn't find any aghori but was amazed by the anger and frustration echoing through the air. Apparently, burning bodies was big business for some and a stressful ordeal for all. I even saw a man and his son diving for leftover jewelry and other treasures in the water, where the remains of wealthy corpses were dumped after roasting for several hours. From day one, I had a visceral love/hate relationship with this city. I was captivated by it nonetheless.

On the bright side, it was dirt cheap to stay there. At the advice of a friend, I landed at Manu's Guest House, a monstrosity of a building with an open-air, central courtyard, decrepit furnishings, a filthy communal bathroom, and a severe monkey problem. Every-so-often an entire army of scraggly, beige and white little monsters would infiltrate the compound, complete with sentries in the stairwells and lookouts on the rooftop. The gang was led by a fearless, alpha-male with egregious eyebrows who would steadily attempt to establish his dominance.

One morning I had just returned from the fruit stand with a bunch of bananas in hand, only to find myself in a standoff with at least twenty such scoundrels. The large male was not deterred by my taunts and had me cornered, squatting down a few feet away where he marked his territory by depositing a tremendous pile of excrement on the floor. As he bared his fangs and hissed at me, the tension reached fever pitch. Suddenly, Manu, a short, stout man in his fifties, charged up the stairs with soap in his hair and wearing only a loincloth. In a rage, he flailed a bamboo pole against the walls.

"HeYa! HeYa!" he screamed, which proved effective in flushing out the intruders. "You've got to show them who is the boss!" he said, gasping for air, before retreating downstairs to finish his shower bucket.

Shenanigans notwithstanding, Manu played host to a rare collection of travelers, many of whom stayed at his guest house long-term and practiced one art form or another—music in particular. Several guests, I learned, rarely left the building, opting instead to stay in their rooms to practice day and night.

One of the guests, Martín, was tall and muscular with high cheekbones and thick black curls. A native of Bolivia, he had traversed Iran and half the Arab world for a year en route to India. On most days, he wore black robes and matching eyeshadow like the *fakirs* (Islamic holy men) he had seen in Pakistan. I found his fashion statement somewhat menacing.

189

Martín spent his days locked in his second-floor room playing harmonium and singing *Sa Re Ga's* (*Do Re Me's* in Hindi) at the top of his lungs. Every now and again he could be heard hollering out, "BOOM, SHIVA!" with such ferocity that it shook the walls and meant he was taking a smoke break. We met one night on the outdoor patio of the third floor, where the majority of the guests stayed, and he generously offered me Afghani hash that he had sewn into his *chappals* (sandals) and had smuggled across two unforgiving borders. He was quite enigmatic but affable enough, and, after a few hours of smoking, we turned in for the night. Prior to heading to bed, I decided to take a shower, as Benares sticks to you like gum on the bottom of your shoe.

As I bathed in the nearly pitch black, monsoon midnight, I began to feel the presence of a force I couldn't see, though in my mind's eye I knew something else was there with me. The delusions continued. I sensed peculiar sounds at odd frequencies. The sounds weren't quite audible, yet, somehow, they were crystal clear. I was still a little afraid of Martín, suspecting that he was some sort of sorcerer—his personality was so commanding. As he had already gone to bed, however, I reasoned that it couldn't be him, or his spirit, taunting me while I washed up.

Suddenly, I perceived a whisper: "*Sheeeevvvvaaaahhhh.*"

I froze, paralyzed by the inaudible sound.

Is it really Shiva, the patron God of Benares? I wondered.

I wasn't sure, nor did I know if I believed in this power. Stephen had occasionally spoken of Shiva with tremendous reverence. The silent voice persisted, speaking in short, penetrating phrases. It directed me to reach down and touch my perineum—the area between one's genitals and one's anus, which is said to be the location of *muladhara*, the root chakra. I resisted with all my might, desperately trying to avoid the area as I washed. But, at some point, it felt as if my hand was no longer my own. My fingers wandered and brushed up against the sensitive patch of skin. Instantly I felt a spark, as if I'd literally lit a match under my ass, and as I caught my breath a powerful energy surged up my spine. My body began to throb with this new current. Panicking, I quickly dried and rushed back to my room, throwing myself under the sheets where I lied shivering with fear.

In the minutes that followed, I tried to make sense of what was happening. I figured that if seven-hundred million Hindus were tuned into a belief in an omnipotent deity, it was possible that it was conscious and possessed that sort of power. Whether an actual, physical deity—personified by the popular image of a strapping, dreadlocked, blue-skinned god draped in a tiger skin—preceded the belief during an ancient, supernatural era, I couldn't say. But, as the classical deity was representative of forces inherent in nature, I reasoned that it was always manifesting in everything.

So, Shiva has moved in, I thought to myself. *Now what?*

Rolling onto my left side, I spotted a sticker on the wall portraying the god Ganesh—Shiva's gregarious son, half-man, half-elephant. Still shaking, I stared at the image, fixating on the various details of Ganesh's appearance and the magnetic draw the icon seemed to have over me. After another minute or so I began to giggle involuntarily. Soon I started to laugh aloud, and a moment later I was in hysterics for apparently no reason at all. Slowly, my tension eased and I felt wonderful, full of joy and almost celebratory. A more benign god had stepped in to save the day! Of the one million deities in Hinduism, only a handful are in the starting line-up—I was fortunate they appeared on stickers and that somebody was kind enough to leave one behind.

Still reeling from this latest conundrum and in need of a break from Benares, I booked an overnight train ride to the border and paid twenty dollars for a visa to enter Nepal. Turning down an offer to buy hashish on the steps of the foreign tourist office, I baked beneath the brutal sun with a handful of grumpy travelers for eight hours before catching a night bus to Kathmandu. There was barely enough room inside the bus to breathe. About two hours into the ride, I ate one of the bhang cookies I'd smuggled out of India and fell fast asleep, waking only in the middle of the night when we stopped to use the restroom and drink Coca-Cola in the streets of some sparkly, junction town. A Buddhist monk in saffron robes who had sat in the row in front of mine approached me smiling with gleaming eyes. I bowed to him. Neither of us said a word, but I sensed that he was in-tune with my pleasant state of mind. Once we were back on-board I could "hear" his silent voice humming a mantra and acknowledging me from his seat, as if we were traveling together.

Thirty-six hours after having left Benares, we pulled into Kathmandu at sunrise. I was surprisingly alert but had no idea how to proceed. Luckily, the monk was headed to the same district where I had planned to stay and invited me to share a taxi. Crashing down at a small guest house within earshot of Boudhanath Stupa—a famous Buddhist shrine—I stowed my belongings, flopped onto the bed and drifted off to sleep.

I began to dream that I was walking in a barren desert beside Michael Franti, the famous yogi-musician who had been at Burning Man the previous summer. As we walked together in the sand, he appeared to be several feet taller than me and had a serene way about him.

"Are we going to do yoga?" I asked.

"You are going to continue traveling," he said, looking me square in the eyes. "Africa will again become a reality. You will be with a woman whose heart you've already touched, and this time it will be okay."

As his image faded, I awoke to the resounding blasts of Tibetan horns, clanging cymbals and hypnotic, Sanskrit chants echoing from nearby monasteries.

In the days that followed I tirelessly roamed the city, climbing stupas, eating *momos* (dumplings), taking photos and climbing to the hotel rooftop to practice yoga for hours on end. Open and receptive, I also came to feel the energy of the monks' frequent serenades, recognizing that their jarring music and mesmerizing prayers were intended to vanquish negative energies and unwanted spirits. I felt renewed.

193

About two weeks removed from my seemingly prognostic dream, on a particularly peaceful afternoon I ventured to a nearby internet café. Opening my email, I found an invitation to join a Birthright trip to Israel—an all-expenses paid excursion for Jewish youths aged eighteen to twenty-six. Though I had never taken much interest in organized religion, I was rapidly approaching my twenty-sixth birthday and knew this would be my last opportunity to take advantage of the Israeli government's generous offer. Upon further investigation I learned that while the tour was ten days long, I could prolong my flight home for up to three months, which would allow me ample time to explore the region on my own. I would leave in January.

I immediately started on the application when, out of the blue, I received an email from Annabelle. In it she spoke of having accepted a teaching position at a small beach resort on the Sinai Peninsula in Egypt, a stone's throw from Israel.

"I'll be there the first of the year," she wrote.

CHAPTER 22
BIRTHRIGHT

I SHOT DOWN TO DELHI and caught the next flight back to New York, arriving in the States after six months abroad. The night after I returned, the Jacob Fred Jazz Odyssey opened for Sound Tribe at a jam-packed theater in Times Square. I had written ahead to the bands' managers who set me up with a backstage pass and a badge for my camera. Hanging around after the show, I realized, for the first time, how much I had changed while I was away. The giddiness and sheer nervousness that I'd previously felt around the musicians had disappeared without a trace, and the paranoia that had been a constant since I'd met Alberto Montana had all but vanished. It was as if I'd shed a skin.

When I got back to Massachusetts, my family's warm welcome was short lived after I spilled the beans about my plans to depart for Israel come January, a mere three months away. My father had been diagnosed with colon cancer shortly after I had left for India. Though he was on the mend, I could feel resentment from both him and my mom, who reminded me that I'd been absent for 9-11 as well. I felt guilty. I wanted to be close to them, but I also believed in what I was doing, even if I couldn't define it and it meant my having to leave.

Despite their lackluster reception, I persuaded my parents to let me stay and set to work processing the fruits of my latest

195

journey—well over a thousand photographs. The Fall zoomed by. I was glued to the computer screen, impelled by the need to create something great, as both my money and my parents' patience were running out.

Immediately after the New Year, I arrived in Israel and boarded a bus full of twenty-somethings on a free vacation. From the start, we were all pleasantly surprised by the accommodations—nice hotels, delicious meals, and even a small wad of cash to spend at our leisure. By day we hiked through some of the country's most stunning landscapes, including Ein Gedi, Galilee, the Dead Sea, and Masada.

Over the course of the ten-day tour, however, our lot was slowly run into the ground by incessant sightseeing. At the brink of our exhaustion, we were overwhelmed by a visit to Jerusalem's melancholic Holocaust museum, Yad Vashem, on *Shabbat*—the Sabbath. After passing through the hallowed halls relatively immune to the imagery, I finally sat down, took a deep breath, and asked the Universe whether any of my ancestors had perished in the concentration camps. As my family was not in touch with their roots, I really didn't know. Instantly, I received an answer.

"You better believe it," said an intuitive voice.

I was overcome with grief and wept uncontrollably.

That same evening, we were treated to a wonderful dinner but not before being bombarded with Zionist propaganda. The men of our group were told exhilarating war stories over free beer, while the women attended a workshop on "How to Make Jewish Babies." We were also required to attend a special service led by a zealous Rabbi and his cohort, who began to sing and encouraged everyone to get up and dance. In that moment I felt tremendous energy emanating from the Rabbi's heart and third eye. Within a minute, much of the group had been swept off their feet and were parading around with him. I was fairly certain that he had knowledge of working with energy, perhaps having studied *Kabbalah*, and had manipulated the group on a subtle level.

While I slept that night, my suspicion was reinforced when one of the members of the Rabbi's team showed up in my dreams attempting to blast me with rainbow light streaming out of his brow, which I instinctively blocked. A few days later, we visited a vineyard in the Golan Heights for a wine tasting when I spotted an interesting painting hanging from the wall of the sampling room. The artwork depicted an old Rabbi with a long, gray beard, black robes, and *tefillin*, a small box containing miniature scriptures tied tightly around his head and forearm. What caught my attention was that the painting also displayed rainbow lights emerging from the Rabbi's forehead.

Upon our release from the program, I spent a couple of blissful days in Tel Aviv, which looked a lot like Madison Avenue only it was by the beach. Reluctantly, I applied for an Egyptian visa so I wouldn't have to deal with earning one at the border. Receiving the stamp in Israel ruined my plans to avoid any traces in my passport of having been there, as such marks prevent a traveler from entering into much of the Arab world. And then, after much anticipation, Annabelle arrived from Sinai. It would be an exaggeration to say that we fell in love immediately. It probably took a day or two.

After dining on olives and feta we'd bought at the elaborate *shouk* (market) and drinking fresh juices to help her get over a cold, we boarded a bus to Eilat, crossed into Egypt without any problems, and continued onto Cairo. We had been invited to stay in a posh apartment on the European-influenced island of Zamalek. We quickly retreated to our room. Our hosts hardly saw us for several days and when we finally came up for air, it was because Annabelle had to get back to work. Traveling southeast by shared taxi, we arrived in Sinai late one night, and she invited me into her small hut in the sand beside the glistening Red Sea.

Life was blissful there, yet my inner guide continually pestered me to return to Cairo to shoot a photo-documentary, which seemed like a reasonable plan of action. I knew Cairo would be cheap, stimulating, and would make for a much better relationship buffer than the transparent mosquito netting that hung in Annabelle's tiny shack. Once I broke the news that I planned to leave, we decided to visit the nearby town of Dahab, a backpacker sand-trap a little further down the coast, to enjoy a few more days together.

Though she was a seasoned festival-goer, Annabelle had minimal traveling experience outside the U.S. We were both a little overwhelmed by all the attention we received from the ambitious restaurant maître d's and trinket sellers that lined the streets of Dahab, pressuring foreigners to buy their goods. Having found a quiet and reliable fast food restaurant, we had taken to eating *foul* (beans)*, tameya* (fried chickpeas) and *tahina* (sesame paste) virtually every meal. While we ate, I did my best to show her the ropes, teaching her to read body language, gauge eye contact, and to sniff out a rat well in advance.

"What do you think, I was born yesterday?" she said. "I'm from Staten Island, remember?"

"I know, I know. I just want to make sure we're on the same page. Never give your money to someone before they provide their service," I warned, "as they might take off with it."

"Got it," she said, mocking me.

One afternoon we set out toward a reclusive beach at the far end of town. En route, we were stopped by a good-looking, Egyptian man named Amir, who was enjoying a smoke at the base of a small hut. We had met Amir a few days earlier when the charming local had struck up a conversation in an effort to lure us into an Italian restaurant. Amir was now on his day off, so we let him be and continued onto the beach, where we stayed a couple hours before retracing our path back to our hotel. When we passed by the small hut, Amir was sitting in the same spot where we'd left him. He invited us to smoke a joint with him.

The lavender sun was setting over the sea, and the mood was just right as he told us stories of his childhood in Alexandria, his extensive education—which included anthropology and philosophy—and his passion for cooking. The latter struck a chord with Annabelle, who was an aspiring chef. We mentioned to Amir that while we were on a tight budget, we had planned to treat ourselves to a nice, fish dinner, as all along the beach we'd seen icy displays full of beautiful catches.

"I have a better idea," said Amir. "I will cook for you! I've done this many times for tourists. It is one of my favorite things! Together we can go to the fish market. I will buy the fish, as they'll give me a better price. Then we can go to my home, and I will prepare a feast for us! You will love it—much better than eating at a restaurant, and much cheaper!"

Annabelle and I talked it over and, as she was excited by the idea of getting into the kitchen alongside Amir, we agreed. Amir kept us thoroughly entertained throughout the walk, telling us wonderful tales about the Bedouins and his own adventures as a horse whisperer in the North country. When we neared the fish market, I gave Annabelle some money and went off on my own to buy a bottle of wine, which Amir suggested would add a nice ambiance to the dish, if not the whole evening.

Reuniting with the two of them, Annabelle proudly displayed the massive, spotted grouper Amir had chosen for our dinner. Our mouths were watering. We followed Amir about a half-mile down the beach to a quiet area where he pointed to what appeared to be an abandoned restaurant.

"I live back there," he said, motioning toward a small, white house with a light on the porch. "And I work at this restaurant, only now it's the off-season so it's closed. The owner lets me use the kitchen when I do special dinners like this. I'll go back there now and get started."

"I was hoping to help you," said Annabelle. "Maybe I can make the salad while you do the fish?"

"Great," replied Amir. "Just wait here while I go to the kitchen to make sure we have everything we need. I'll be back in a few minutes with a couple glasses of wine for you to enjoy while the fish is cooking."

As we watched Amir dash into the kitchen with the grouper and the wine, I had a sudden, sinking feeling in the pit of my stomach. We had spent well over a thousand pounds on the meal—over twenty U.S. dollars—which was a small fortune in Egypt, yet here we were waiting on a deserted stretch of beach as the mosquitoes arrived in droves. After forty-five minutes our stomachs were growling, but there was no sign of Amir.

"I'm sure it just took him a little longer than expected to get things going," said Annabelle.

After an hour I began to lose my cool and, despite Amir's instructions to stay put, I decided to venture into the kitchen to see what was going on. Needless to say, the place was completely empty. There wasn't even a stove, let alone a cook. When I told Annabelle, her face dropped. Together, we set out toward the white house where Amir had said he lived. Since no one was home, we called out to some of his neighbors and one of them came over to engage us. Earlier that afternoon I had taken Amir's portrait, and, as I still had my camera on me, it occurred to me to show the man the picture. He laughed aloud when he saw it.

"Does this man live here?" we asked.

"You saw this man?" he chuckled. "This man is not living here. This man is liar. Liar! Do not trust this man!"

Our faces turned beet red. Annabelle was speechless. I was furious. We made a b-line for the Italian restaurant. Upon finding it closed, we stopped in a bar across the street.

"Do you know this guy?" I asked the owner, flashing him the picture.

"Yes, he used to work here but he was fired. Did you give him money?"

I didn't answer but, from my silence, the owner knew I had. Likewise, judging by his half-smirk, I knew he'd seen it all before.

"Where can we find him?" I pleaded.

"He is gone. Better you go home."

Still fuming, I insisted to Annabelle that we go to the police station. Our sense was that none of the locals were going to give him up, and I wanted justice. The police, however, were notorious for beating perpetrators and, even if they decided to help us, would only make matters worse.

At the height of my anger, I decided to surrender. Our hunger won out, and we hightailed it to the fast food joint where we spent less than a buck on huge plates of eggs and fried lentils. As the stinging feeling of having been sucker-punched slowly subsided, it dawned on us that we had been privy to a remarkable feat of artistry. Amir had played us like a lyre, and for that he deserved the fish *and* the wine. Hopefully he was enjoying his feast at a nice, quiet spot, maybe even with someone special. When we finished our dinner, we made up our minds to depart first thing in the morning.

"Fucking Dahab," said Annabelle, shaking her head in disgust before bursting into hysterics. We laughed so hard we nearly hit the floor.

*   *   *

At the crack of dawn, we kissed each other goodbye and boarded separate buses. Hours later in Cairo, I managed to hunt down the cheapest hostel—ironically, called the Hotel Dahab—in the tourist district near Tahir Square. With little effort, I found a comparable fast food restaurant practically within earshot and got back to work taking photography walks around the city. I drank *cha* (tea) or *irfa*—hot milk loaded with cinnamon—at one sidewalk café after another. In time, I grew close with a clique of Sudanese refugees, all of whom were artists and played football (soccer) with the ex-pats on the weekends. Life was good.

When Annabelle came to visit a couple weeks later, we took a train to Alexandria and an overnight bus to Siwa, a genuine oasis in the desert near the Libyan border. Sadly, the oasis had been spoiled by tourism and was decidedly dreary. From the moment we arrived, Annabelle felt uncomfortable on account of the virulent looks she received from some of the local men. As a consequence, we spent much of our time in our hotel room eating chocolate-covered dates by the kilo, as this was the most accessible food in town.

Annabelle's morale steadily declined. On our last day we went looking for a hot spring on the edge of the Saharan dunes and accidentally wandered into a private garden. Calling out to the owner, we were greeted by a smiling, middle-aged Egyptian man named Mohammed. He graciously took us on a tour of his orchard, which included several olive and fig trees, lemons, oranges, dates, hibiscus and even green vegetables, all of them thriving via a natural aqueduct he had channeled out of the desolate, sandy earth. As we walked, we enjoyed a bag of special dates he had picked and washed for us, yet we had the sense we were being watched. We heard a giggle and turned to see a little girl who, embarrassed, raced over and tugged on Mohammed's dusty gray *galabiya*. Then came another girl, and another one slightly older, and another, and another. There were seven sisters in total, one more radiant than the next, and the overwhelming pride evidenced by Mohammed's bright red cheeks restored Annabelle's faith in humanity and salvaged our trip together.

It was several weeks before she returned to Cairo to visit me again. One evening we were walking down the street when I ducked into a store to buy some chocolate. I heard her scream. I dashed to her side.

"That guy just groped me!" she cried out.

I looked down the block to see a shady figure streaking away toward the corner and started after him, screaming as loud as I could. After a few feet, however, I stopped running as I never would've caught him, had no intention of beating him, and knew Annabelle needed me. Her legs gave out and she collapsed onto the sidewalk in tears. I helped her up and we rushed to a friend's home nearby. It took several hours before she was able to even talk about the incident. Even then, there was little I could do to console her. It was her last night in town, and our visit ended on a sour note. In the morning she headed back to Sinai to resume her teaching duties.

My last few weeks in Cairo were spent in one of the city's seediest areas, Saida Zenab, stalking a photo story on illegal street butchers. I had no reason to focus on this topic other than that a fellow traveler had mentioned it would be a visually stunning and politically-charged experience, as the butchers and the community had recently been dealt a blow by the Egyptian government. Local officials and wealthy builders had decided to erect a new hospital a few hundred meters from the livestock marketplace, which had been there since time immemorial. The powers that be had ordered the marketplace shut down over concerns about sanitation. The butchers, meanwhile, had continued to operate clandestinely, at least with regard to slaughtering their animals in broad daylight, and were regarded as a rough-and-tumble bunch. In other words, this was not the sort of place that showed up on the tourist maps.

In an effort to capture the ambiance of the scene, I would arrive early in the morning to eat *foul* (pronounced, "fool") from a street vendor, one of hundreds around town that served up hot beans and eggs with *baladi* bread for hordes of hungry, Egyptian men on their way to work. Another expat friend from Tunisia had challenged me to seek out the "most powerful" *foul*, and I was certain this stuff was the best. All was well until one morning when a crazed local grabbed my arm and reached for my camera, demanding that I leave the area as I didn't belong there. Fortunately, a handful of young men came to my aid and laughed at the assailant, explaining to me in Arabic and with the use of hand gestures that he was "not right in the head."

With my belly full, I would proceed to the market and shadow anyone I could until they'd inevitably bark at me to get lost. One sheepherder, however, noticed the Buddhist prayer beads I had picked up in Nepal and wore around my wrist. Thinking they were Muslim prayer beads like his own, he let me photograph him as he praised Allah. The moment became surreal when *Adan*, the ethereal call to prayer, began to blare from loud speakers all across town as if the herder, with his arms raised high toward the heavens, had conjured it himself.

Over the course of a few days, I watched bloodied workers rummage through assorted cow parts in the pouring rain; was briefly locked in a pen with a lovely heifer that tried to kiss me; and, was yelled at and demoralized countless times by any number of surly butchers, some of whom even threatened to dispose of me. But, for every mean episode there was a ray of light, like the young boys that let me follow them on their daily chores; a group of herders who shared their lunch with me; and, a crazy, toothless drunk who pretended to talk on a broken mobile phone and had us all in stitches.

Finally, on my last morning in Cairo, a pair of young men who had let me sit with them day after day as they waited for a sale, beckoned me into their dark stall. A customer had arrived and laid down money in exchange for a sheep. The room went completely silent other than the sound of the butcher sharpening his knife against a stone. I watched in awe as the merciless hand of Death descended upon us, lifted and slammed the sheep to the ground, and, in a matter of seconds, slit its throat and drained the life out of the unsuspecting animal. The sheep's blood steamed as it spilled across the floor.

The butchers wasted no time hanging the carcass, skinning it from head to toe, packaging it and tossing it in the back of a pickup truck. When the customer had pulled away, the pair sat back and had a smoke, counted their money and posed for numerous photographs, each of them sporting a look of cold-blooded pride.

Chapter 23
The Blue Light

At the beginning of April 2007, I returned to the U.S. from Tel Aviv, having flown on my 27th birthday. In total, I had spent three months in the desert and nine of the previous twelve abroad. I felt like I had made contact with my Jewish heritage, which I hadn't anticipated, had built a solid portfolio of photographs, and had fallen in love with Annabelle yet again.

Before leaving Israel, I had celebrated Passover with relatives in Jerusalem—essentially the Jewish equivalent of the Hajj pilgrimage to Mecca. Upon touching down at JFK, I headed straight to my brother's home in Brooklyn for the second night of the holiday, snapping photos all along the way. Captivated by the dramatic shift in scenery and culture, I arrived at his place at sunset to greet my entire family, some of whom I hadn't seen since before I had left for Oregon over two years prior. They all drank *slivovitz* (Hungarian whiskey)—a tried and true tradition among the clan—and fudged through a considerably lax ceremony (in comparison) before indulging in a variety of rich chicken and beef dishes. After everyone had gone home or passed out, I temporarily moved into a small room that doubled as a storage closet.

While riding the bus in Manhattan one afternoon, I got a call about a part-time job assisting a professional dog photographer, an opportunity I jumped on as it meant experience and income, albeit minimum wage. When I received another call about a cheap room in Astoria, Queens, I leaped at that as well. Within a few hours, I relocated to Ditmars Boulevard and settled into a grungy, old house full of artists and musicians—a New York version of Manu's Guest House, minus the monkeys.

Each day I rode the N train to Union Square and walked twenty-five minutes to a small, in-house photo studio in the depths of the East Village. My boss was designing a book he had been commissioned to shoot featuring dogs wearing lingerie. My job was to handle his correspondence, run the occasional errand, manage the lights, and captivate the dogs while we attempted to get them to smile for the camera. Most of the dogs were pint-sized, agreeable and easily manipulated—the sorts of pets that were used to playing dress-up with their zany owners. My last assignment, however, was to convince a two-hundred-pound American Mastiff pup named "Tank" to wear a speedo and stand on his hind legs. I actually succeeded in doing this by teasing him with a tennis ball before he came crashing down on me and slobbered a reservoir of drool across my face.

Still beats the law firm, I reminded myself.

In the middle of June, about six weeks into the job, I was walking to the subway in the late afternoon when I spotted an exceptionally tall, shirtless young man holding up a large sign in the middle of Union Square Park. He looked like an antenna, and upon closer inspection I made out his slogan: *Famous*

209

Spiritual Healer, Over 20,000 Healed, Will Take Away Your Pain. In smaller print the sign also read, *6'7-inch Jew, Will Rap for Food.* Intrigued, I approached the towering figure, who introduced himself as Te'Devan "Rocketman" Kurzweil.

"Formerly 'Jeremy from New Jersey,'" he told me, "before I met an old Chinese *qigong* master who turned my world upside-down."

"What, exactly, do you do?" I asked.

"Let me show you."

Placing his giant sign on the ground, he backed away about ten feet, steadied his body, and began to manipulate my energy field with subtle hand gestures and deep breathing, as if he'd suddenly become a channel for a higher power. I stood frozen, my mind fixated on the peculiar sensation of knots being untied on the right side of my belly.

"I'm cleaning out your liver," he confirmed without my having to ask.

Then, bending backward slightly, he threw his head back, spread his massive arms like albatross wings and let out a loud, high-pitched "*heeee-uuuuuuuueeeeeee*" sound that sent energy spinning through the crown of my head. I was speechless. When he finished, he moved to about six inches from me and, still spellbound, I offered him an apple as compensation while silently kicking myself for not having met him sooner. Above all else, he served as an unexpected reminder that I was not back in the city to be a photographer's assistant or a dog handler.

In July, my work with the "Phodographer" dried up, and I vowed to give it a go on my own. Annabelle returned from Egypt just in time to keep me company. She settled in Staten Island, but we spent nearly every night together. We made plans to attend Burning Man at the end of the summer.

A month later, I landed my first sizeable gig—a photo shoot for an urban gardener. Things were looking up, though I was working seven days a week and losing sleep due to the stress of wheeling and dealing.

Eager for a break herself, Annabelle took time off from her job as a barista and visited me at my parents' home in Massachusetts. My folks were out of town, and I had been up there prepping my print portfolio and pitching stories without much success. While I was initially glad to see her, within a couple days of her arrival I was itching to get back to work. As she was planning to quit the coffee shop in order to start bartending, it became apparent that our lifestyles were diverging. I had already bought her a plane ticket to Nevada for the Burn, but on the last night of her visit I sat down to work while she slept. It was then that my "guide," who had been relatively quiet in recent weeks, accosted me.

"What the hell are you doing!?" blared the mysterious, silent voice inside my mind. "She's holding you back! You've wasted this whole week! You need to let her go!"

My forehead was throbbing, and anxiety set in like a cold, uncomfortable fog. As much as I hated to admit it, the voice was right. She and I were prolonging the inevitable.

In the morning, when she tried to lay her head on my chest, all I could do was stare at the ceiling.

"What's wrong?" she said.

"I think you love me more than I love you."

*   *   *

We decided to go to Burning Man separately. I felt a gut-wrenching guilt for having broken her heart so many times in an effort to follow my own. I left for Portland ten days early to meet up with Tristan. Everything was up in the air.

In Portland, I was greeted by ominous clouds. I headed directly to the home of a stranger I had met on the internet a day earlier in an effort to buy a bicycle for the playa. Expecting a piece of junk, for twenty dollars he handed me a sturdy, black dirt bike with brand new, fat white tires supporting a frame painted with butterflies and covered with alien stickers.

The perfect bike for Burning Man, I thought.

From there I rode downhill along a busy boulevard with my heavy backpack on, then hopped back on the metro for another thirty minutes to the far end of town. The moment I hit the streets again, it started pouring. I pedaled my way to Tristan's studio, an additional ten minutes ride. I was thoroughly drenched by the time I knocked on his door, but he welcomed me with open arms. After showing me his new clothing designs, he sewed psychedelic patches on a fuzzy vest he gave me to combat the cold.

After the skies cleared, I rode to Stephen's house, excited
to meet my teacher after a year and-a-half absence. When I
arrived he made chai, offered me some "*OM*-grown" pot, as he
put it, and we sat on his back porch catching up. As I excitedly
went on and on about my newfound success as an artist, he
unexpectedly shot me a look of utter disdain. There was also
something disconcerting about his cockeyed gaze. In his pupils
I swore I saw Shiva and felt the same eerie presence that had
haunted me in Benares. Instantly, his whole demeanor changed.
I was seized by fear, overcome with shame, and intuited that I
was headed in the wrong direction.

"You got that right," he scoffed, reading my thoughts.
"You're missing the whole thing, bro."

I was totally dumbstruck.

"Didn't you learn anything?" he said.

I knew he was alluding to my time in India, and an image
of Swami Gopeshwarananda flashed through my mind.

"Yeah, you blew that one, too!" he said.

Again, he'd read my thoughts.

"That was the best thing you had going for you," he added.

"Well, what am I supposed to do?" I said.

I was visibly shaken and embarrassed. Another image
crossed my mind: I saw myself sitting peacefully in a tree in
the Berkshires.

"That's a start," said Stephen. "And what the hell are you
doing out here?"

I envisioned Tristan, my campmates and the chaotic scene
at Burning Man.

213

"You like playing dress-up, huh? It ain't nothin' compared to the *Kumbh Mela!*" He shook his head in disapproval as my confidence continued to plummet.

"How do you know all this?" I asked, stupefied.

"Come on, bro," he retorted, "I've been surfing the *paramatrix* for years!"

Over the course of an hour with Stephen, my entire life plan was completely dismantled, and a radically different vision for the future began to emerge. When I rose to leave, his bizarre expression shifted again. As if nothing unusual had happened, we said goodbye.

"Your medicine doesn't always taste good," he said, as I rode away.

At Burning Man, I felt out of place and was disappointed by how much it seemed to have changed, or how much I had changed, since my previous visit there two years earlier. My most pleasant moments were those spent alone in the quietude of the desert.

After the Burn, I hitched to San Francisco. While waiting on the side of the road, a service truck ran over my prized, aluminum coffee thermos with a sticker of Ganesh on it, officially ending the party. Passersby tossed me granola bars and warm cans of beer before I was picked up by a maniacal twenty-year old who drove a hundred miles-per-hour. He anxiously seized up each time his police-radar, which he claimed gave him "peace of mind," sounded on the dashboard. I bit my lip as he ranted about his week of drug-induced sexcapades and all the bliss he felt inside.

After a few days in the Bay, I headed back to New York to face the music. I photographed charity events and weddings, ran into the streets during snowstorms to try to get news coverage, took pictures of car accidents and came up with fantasy travel assignments that I pitched to the editors, editors' assistants and even the coffee girls at all the local periodicals. I almost never heard back, then one day I caught a break.

It was a cold Saturday in November. I had plans to meet with a patron who had commissioned several fine art prints and, serendipitously, landed a job with the Village Voice photographing the annual Burning Man "Decompression" party at the Queens Museum. Suddenly, I had enough money to live on.

That morning I practiced yoga on the carpet in the center of my bedroom. In closing, I lied down for an extended yoga nidra relaxation, just like Stephen had taught me to do. For reasons unbeknownst to me, I slipped into an extraordinarily deep meditative state. After several minutes of feeling energy swirling through my body, a blissful calm passed over me. Suddenly, I felt a unique pressure in the center of my skull. In the next instance, an orb of blue light miraculously emerged from my forehead and hovered like a bubble in front of my eyes.

"Why don't you start a school?" said a mysterious, unfamiliar, silent voice in a soft tone, as if speaking from right beside me.

Of course, that's what I should do. It was as if I'd known it all along.

Chapter 24
The Stand

WITH WINTER CLOSING IN, my gig with the Village Voice had solidified. Feeling confident, I invested in leather, hardbound portfolios that I filled with my best work and dropped off at all the major magazines in New York City. Despite my love for my craft, the chaotic pace, fierce competition, and nonstop hustle of the art world was rapidly taking its toll. The tension was amplified at night, and I began to experience full-blown insomnia. Stephen's warning that I was on the wrong path echoed through my mind.

With the holidays approaching, I reached out to Sound Tribe in an effort to photograph their New Year's run in Atlanta. A few nights later they came to me in a vivid dream disguised as multicolored leopards, lions, and tigers, sniffing me up and down.

"He's cool," declared one of them. "We can have him along."

The next morning, I received an email inviting me as a VIP so I could "share [my] energy," as they put it. I was honored by their gesture and proud that they had accepted me into their inner circle after all those years. During the shows, I was able to move as I pleased throughout the arena and felt respected for my craft. Backstage, I never quite felt at home. I was there to do a job and was increasingly disillusioned by the scene and my role within it.

After the crescendo performance on New Year's Eve, I left the venue by myself and began to wander the streets of downtown Atlanta, still crawling with tipsy revelers in funny hats. Pausing to stretch on a quiet corner, I was amazed to spot a familiar face.

"Jonathan!"

It was Coretta's boyfriend. He was heading straight for me. We hadn't seen each other since we'd strolled along the bluff with Coretta after she had emerged from her coma. He looked the same—tall and thin with wise, hazel eyes, only his hair was a little longer.

"Wow!" he said.

He was with some friends, having just left Widespread Panic's show, which had been nearby.

"How was the show?" I asked.

"It was awesome! How about yours?"

"Pretty cool." I showed him the photo of the ecstatic crowd that I'd snapped from the behind the stage as hundreds of balloons dropped from the ceiling at the stroke of midnight.

"Impressive," he said.

"Not nearly as incredible as seeing you here! Happy New Year! Please send my love to Coretta. I can't wait to see her."

"Will do," he said. His eyes twinkled ever-so-briefly before disappearing into the night.

Inspired, I started in the opposite direction when I was seized by an inexplicable sensation. I could hear Jonathan's silent voice talking to me in my mind, as if our conversation had continued even after we'd parted.

"Coretta sent me to check on you," said the voice. "It's time for you to move on from Sound Tribe Sector 9. Remember, focus on what *you're* doing."

Suddenly, a powerful blast of hot, white light shot down from the sky and zapped me in the center of my forehead in several short, jarring bursts. The impact nearly knocked me over. Completely entranced, as the shock subsided I felt euphoric and exceptionally lucid. In retrospect, I wasn't sure whether a purifying light had entered me or if I had been unplugged from a large energy field, presumably that of the concert scene. Either way, the experience was akin to a spiritual rebirth. It was a genuine miracle, and a stark reminder of where I'd come from, where I was going and whom I was really traveling with.

My guardian angel, I thought. *She's been with me all along.*

I slept-in the following morning. Sometime around dawn, I was visited by Stephen in a strikingly vivid dream. He spoke to me as if he were sitting right beside me.

"This is the year!" he said, emphatically. "Everything will change. You're going to return to India, although this time you'll have no need for your tent. How's *that* for a New Year's resolution!"

In my mind's eye, I saw myself walking jovially along the streets of Benares and could hear him laughing in the background. When I awoke I was ecstatic to have received such an explicit message. It was the sort of prophecy I could build my life around, which is exactly what I did.

Two days later, I was visiting family in the Berkshires when I received a call from my roommate in Queens.

"The landlord has decided to move his family into our house," he said. "We've got to be out by March."

I took it as a sign that my days in New York were numbered, and it was time to shift gears. I felt relieved. Moments later, the phone rang again. This time it was the head of a local art school calling to ask my father for a contribution. Seizing the opportunity to introduce myself, I explained to her that I was an artist from the city considering a move to the area and looking to teach. She offered me a job at their children's summer camp on the spot. We didn't talk details, but I assumed the job would pay me enough to justify a permanent move to the country. Since everything was tentative, I decided not to share the news with my folks and went back to the grind for a few more months.

On March 1st, after a successful photo shoot for New York Magazine and my most difficult assignment with the Village Voice—in which I spent two full days getting threatened and thrown out of a handful of New York's dingy, Off-Track Betting parlors—I packed up my room in Astoria, borrowed a friend's pickup truck, and retreated to my parents' home.

They knew I was coming, though the reality of the situation didn't sink in for them until I pulled into their driveway with all my stuff. I had been in-and-out of their place for months at a time since finishing college, so they weren't surprised to see me back. This time was clearly different, however, and they did little to mask their displeasure. We remained cordial until dinner that evening.

"So, what's your plan?" they asked.

I swallowed my pride.

"With your permission, I'd like to stay here for a couple weeks to help prune the apple trees and save some money. In April, I'll head south for a music festival and to visit Coretta. Then I'll come back in May to rent a place nearby and help with the garden."

My father groaned, shaking his head and escalating the tension.

"I assume you intend to stay here in May, too, while you're looking for a place?" he said.

"I hope to have it sorted out by then. But, yes, I may need to stay for a bit if I can't find something right away."

"So, your plan is to live up here?" he said, raising his voice. "There's nothing happening up here! No money. No jobs. You know we'd never kick you out, but it's not good for you to stay here. We're done raising kids, and things are just getting going for you in the city. Don't you see that you're continually running away from success? Every time you start to build some momentum, you move onto the next thing. First it was the law firm, then your sales job out West, and now this. You're letting fear dictate the course of your life. Can't you see that?"

"You're twenty-eight years old," added my mother. "Do you think you're going to live here with us forever? Doesn't that embarrass you, to live with your parents? Don't you want to get married, get a real job, and have kids of your own?"

My face sunk, but I refused to back down.

"No, it doesn't embarrass me at all," I said. "I love it here and am doing what I need to do to continue to grow. You haven't been through what I've been through. You haven't seen what I've seen. I haven't been running away! I've been moving forward!"

In truth, I had never once considered that I might be dodging responsibility or running away from anything. I felt liberated and, particularly at this stage, much more in-tune with how I wanted to live my life. I also felt guilty for leveraging my parents' hospitality so often. I'd gone to the well one too many times, and it was coming to a head.

"I was hoping you'd be excited for me," I said, "and happy that I'll be nearby and can lend a hand around here. Throughout most of the world, the whole family lives together and takes care of one another. We're the ones that have it backward."

"No, Son, you've got it backward. We think you're making a terrible mistake," said my father, chiding me. My mother hid her eyes.

In the past, I'd always honored my father.

"Fuck you!" I shouted. "You don't know what's best for me! Only I know what's best for me!"

We all sat motionless amidst a deafening silence. Even the clocks stopped ticking. When he didn't bark back, a smile began to curl across my face. I bit my lower lip to conceal the laughter that had bubbled up from my belly. My whole body tingled as my heart celebrated. I began to cry tears of joy.

Standing up to my parents, and especially to my father, was a rite of passage. I loved them and was grateful for everything they had given me, but I was prepared to go it alone. I left the argument assuming I would trudge back to New York the following day to couch-surf for a couple weeks before my road trip. In the morning, I was finishing up work in the studio when my father knocked on the door.

"Your mother and I talked things over last night," he said. "We've decided we want you to stay, and we're sorry for not trusting you."

I wasn't sure what had shifted in them. It was evident they were worried for me, maybe even pitied me, or couldn't stand the thought of my bouncing around aimlessly for another month. Perhaps they thought about how much it would cost them to hire someone to prune the apple trees. Maybe they had really begun to trust me. Either way, I accepted their apology but didn't give them an inch regarding what they had said the previous night.

"The most valuable thing you can do for me is to believe in me," I said.

That same afternoon I pulled an old ladder and a pair of shears out of the barn and set to work in the orchard. The mangled trees were already thick with suckers and damp with melting snow. The work was cumbersome, but the air was cool and sweet. Completely invested in each branch, I relished the soothing winds of Spring brushing against my cheek and listened to song birds rustle through the surrounding woods. Crawling from the ladder into a tree and resting against the trunk, I breathed deeply and allowed my mind to wander back over all my travels.

I reminisced over the remarkable people I had met and felt tremendous gratitude for all the help I had received along the way. Mostly, I paused to appreciate the brilliant symphony of nature, and realized this was the true teaching I had received. Soon, a new sensation welled up in the depths of my being. An unsurpassed peacefulness washed over me. For the first time in my life, I was *home*.

*   *   *

Arriving beneath the towering live oaks in Savannah, I greeted Coretta for the first time in nearly five years. Throughout that period, she had continued to work diligently with doctors and therapists, relearning how to stand and walk on her own over short distances. She had also improved upon several cognitive functions including her speech, though it remained difficult to understand her. Her short-term memory was still impaired, and she had an awful time recollecting the past, including our experiences together. Despite her setbacks, she remained joyful and humorous, cracking jokes and bursting into laughter every chance she could.

Perhaps the most telling aspects of that visit were the stories of her nurses, a handful of women who had cared for her full-time for over half-a-decade. As we chatted, each of them confessed to me individually that they believed they had found their calling upon meeting Coretta. One of them even confided that Coretta had helped her awaken latent healing abilities.

"Sometimes the Holy Spirit will take over my body and pour out through my hands when I'm with her," she said. "There's something special about that girl."

Strolling along the bluff—me on foot, her in a wheelchair, and the emerald, Spanish moss swaying gently overhead—I marveled at all that Coretta had inspired.

"Are you aware of the impact you've had on us?" I asked her.

"Dunno," she said, shrugging her shoulders.

A few minutes passed before she spoke again.

"How did we meet?" she said.

"We met in Belize," I answered. "On the beach. We nearly fell in love, and then we found each other at Bonnaroo amidst a sea of 100,000 people."

We had already been through this routine several times, but it didn't bother me at all.

"Tell me the story," she said.

"It's a *long* story."

Looking back at me, she rolled her eyes and smiled mischievously.

"We've got all of eternity," she said.

I shook my head, and, with that, I began.

ACKNOWLEDGEMENTS

I WOULD LIKE TO THANK everyone that inspired me to write this book, as well as everyone that continues to encourage me to share my gifts with the world. It's been a long road, but it's been a beautiful one. I would especially like to thank my family for their love, faith, and support. I wish to extend a debt of gratitude to Sarah Fader, who helped breathe life back into this project after several years of dormancy. The help of my editor, Elise Ghitman, has been invaluable and has made me a better writer. Thank you to Claire Gillman for your candid advice, and to Catherine Moncayo and Anna Sims for all your feedback. I am grateful for my peers and mentors in the Department of Psychology at the University of West Georgia, who believed in me and rekindled my imagination time and time again. Lastly, thank you to everyone that supported the book's launch by contributing to the crowdfunding campaign. You've helped me realize a dream; I only hope I can return the favor.